TEACHERS AT WORK
IN THE
ELEMENTARY SCHOOL

TEACHERS AT WORK
IN THE
ELEMENTARY SCHOOL

BY

ALICE M. MEEKER

PATERSON STATE COLLEGE

Illustrated by Robert Tanner

THE **BOBBS-MERRILL** COMPANY, INC.
A SUBSIDIARY OF HOWARD W. SAMS & CO., INC.
Publishers • INDIANAPOLIS • NEW YORK

TO MY PARENTS

Every class is different from every other class; every student of yours is different from all other students; and you are different from every other teacher. It is unusual, therefore, for you to be able to apply anything exactly as you read it, or for you to be able to imitate in every detail a lesson or procedure that you saw used so effectively by another teacher with another class.

Harry N. Rivlin, *Teaching Adolescents in Secondary Schools.* 2nd ed. New York, Appleton-Century Crofts, 1961, p. 434.

Contents

TEACHERS AT WORK
IN THE
ELEMENTARY SCHOOL

Introduction

This little book is meant to be a mixture of ideas and ideals, for one must always complement the other. As teachers, our business is children. Part of this "swift and solemn trust of life" passes through our hands; here we find the adults of tomorrow. As the adults become, so will be our nation in a complex and demanding world.

Elementary teaching is the basis of all teaching, in the same way that first-grade reading underlies upper-grade reading. Reading is a specific subject with tangible goals that can be measured by testing, but teaching has no gauge by which it can be measured, for it involves affection and responsibility. That's why a teacher can't be replaced by a teaching machine.

A teacher's affection for her class sets the climate, and the children respond accordingly. If she is a firm, wise and loving human being, her pupils will be relaxed and happy. Add teaching techniques and ingenuity to such a person, and you will have almost an ideal. But take away that warmth of personality and the little sympathetic extras that are never found in an educational textbook, and you have only efficiency. It's a little like the difference between a steam radiator and an open fireplace: both give out heat, but a fireplace lends more charm to the room. Ideally, the room would be more comfortable if it had both; neither is quite adequate alone.

There's a familiar story to illustrate the point. A lazy student who knew that his professor always read the morning lecture decided to use a tape-recorder instead of going to class. Thus, he could replay the lecture at his leisure and still get some extra sleep. One by one, other students followed his example. One morning the professor cleaned his glasses, adjusted his notes, and perceived with amazement that he had thirty-five receptive tape-recorders in front of him. He finished his lecture and went home. The next morning he arrived with his own tape recorder, turned it on, and left the room. Here was information automatically given and automatically recorded. There was no affection at all, none given and none received.

Affection involves individuals and the constant interplay of personalities. But, in a classroom, responsibility belongs to the teacher —legally, to be sure, but also in a moral sense. Children at this age are too young to have ideals of their own; a child's thinking reflects the thinking of adults, and he is exposed to his teacher about thirty hours a week. A classroom is a small but potent autocracy in which children follow directions and fall under the approval or disapproval of the teacher. How that teacher thinks is important.

Passive acceptance of the teacher's wisdom is easy to most boys and girls. It involves no effort of independent thought, and seems rational because the teacher knows more than his pupils; it is moreover the way to win the favor of the teacher unless he is a very exceptional man. Yet the habit of passive acceptance is a disastrous one in later life. It causes men to seek a leader, and to accept as a leader whoever is established in that position.[1]

This sense of moral responsibility helps a teacher make the decision between what is essential and what is relatively unimportant. In the lower grades, this may encompass the gradual development of initiative, perseverance, and integrity in a group situation, integrated into the reading, science, and arithmetic lessons; in the upper grades, intellectual curiosity, empathy for others, and moral courage are fostered through the guidance of the classroom teacher. In these areas, children are the silent evaluating group: they see, they listen, they select—ideas, attitudes, ideals. The teacher has a great deal to do with the shaping of tomorrow's citizens.

Basic as these concepts are, they are not all-sufficient. Teaching demands knowledge and skill. Here is the purpose of this book. There are good, honest tricks in any trade, and any teacher worthy of the name needs a whole bagful. Primary skills are refined and developed up to and through the sixth grade. A child who starts

[1] Bertrand Russell, "Education." In *Selected Papers of Bertrand Russell*, no. 137. New York, Modern Library, 1927, p. 107.

with sounds and single rhyming words in first grade uses these same skills in attacking the difference between "injure" and "inure" or between "Pacific" and "specific," grades and years later. Two and two make four in first grade, but little by little 1.25 plus 2.75 also emerges as four, in sixth grade. Each year and each skill builds on the previous one. When a child fails to understand an involved problem, it is necessary to return to the simpler form in order to make the transition clear and easy. It is almost essential that the upper-grade teacher have an understanding of primary teaching, for always there will be pupils in upper and middle grades who can learn only by the simplest methods, if they learn at all.

This book should serve as a reminder that children, *per se*, have changed very little, and the best discipline comes from an old-fashioned recipe:

Pour in equal parts *anticipation* and *preparation*;
add *eight hours sleep* for the teacher, before teaching;
season with *a sense of humor*;
and use sufficient *resourcefulness* to keep the mixture from becoming lumpy!

This book should offer bits of provocative thinking for a class in the middle grades. "What makes water wet?" A discussion like this on an appropriately rainy day would involve the "wetter-water" solutions often used by firemen in fighting grass fires; or water off a duck's back; or the use of soap in washing greasy hands. Perhaps even the wetting qualities of mercury, that metallic fluid, may resemble water. Suggestions such as these are only spurs to further ingenuity on the part of a good teacher.

Here, we hope you will find practical help for your overworked moments, some bits of philosophical thinking for your gloomy days, and some fresh approaches to familiar but very necessary work.

CHAPTER 1

Two Feet Well Planted

This is a true story with suspense, climax, and a happy ending. Every experienced teacher will understand it. A young teacher who loved her second-grade class and her job was busy with her pupils one afternoon when there was a knock on the door and little red-haired Ray from the third grade came in. He handed her a pair of scissors. "My teacher said to give these to you, and you could return them to Miss Alberton." Our teacher stopped for a moment to think. These were not her scissors, and why should she return them to the first-grade teacher? Ah-h-h. She knew now. This was her colleague's way of telling her that the county superintendent was visiting the class-rooms.

Panic washed over her for a moment, and then resignation. She sent the scissors to Miss Alberton and went on with the lesson.

When the great man entered and slid into a seat in the back, she scarcely paused. One reading group finished its work and she began a game with the entire class; the visitor had been forgotten. But later there was a note on her desk. It said, "I think you could even make an interesting lesson out of a straight pin!"

She was an excellent teacher, and her county superintendent had recognized this. He had given her the ultimate compliment.

A superior teacher must be ingenious, drawing from a wide store of peripheral knowledge. He or she must be dramatic, pulling fasci-nating tidbits of information from that knowledge. He must be stimulating, encouraging students to read for further information. Let's take the straight pin. How could this become a hypothetical lesson?

STRAIGHT PINS

Have a sufficient stock of straight pins on hand for each of the pupils to have at least one to examine. (It might be advisable to keep an eye on the activities of mischievous boys with original ideas at this point.)

1. List the uses of pins.
2. What did people do before we had them? The Indians, for example?
3. What materials are used to manufacture pins? A magnet will demonstrate simple metal differences.
4. Pins can be used for a counting lesson in basic arithmetic.
5. Write a story about a pin.
6. Who invented safety pins?
7. (*Upper grades*) What does this line from *Hamlet* mean?
   "I do not set my life at a pin's fee."
8. (*Upper grades*) Use of "pin" in various parts of speech.
   She *pinned* the flower to her dress.
   This is a *pin* box.
   Do you have a *pin*?

A stone is an even more fascinating teaching topic than a pin. Is it a pebble smooth and round from the action of water? Has it the well-defined layers of sedimentary rock that has lain under the sea for thousands of years? Has it bits of fossils, touches of quartz, a sprinkle of garnets, or the shimmer of mica? Is it igneous, extruded from the fiery furnaces of the earth, or metamorphic—or a form of ore? Or just slag? And remember that David killed Goliath with a stone; that the Indians used stone for arrowheads; that before the Iron Age there was the Stone Age. Consider the historical values of Plymouth Rock, the Rock of Gibraltar, the Blarney Stone, the Stone of Scone.

A good teacher can use a straight pin, a common stone, a glass of water, anything!—and have a fascinating lesson.

Let's take another hypothetical lesson with a stone. The teacher, like all good teachers, is an inveterate collector of unusual objects.

This time he has a large irregular chunk of dark, heavy lava from which he intends to teach a lesson to his sixth-grade class.

Before school opens, the materials for the lesson are ready and the desk has been cleared. On it have been placed the mysterious rock, a magnet, a compass, and an assortment of small objects. At this point it is well to remember that teaching children to think is the primary task of any teacher. Facts are isolated truths until they fit into the meaning of all life through the medium of the individual mind. There is satisfaction in this discovery, for at this point facts become knowledge. If the teacher understands this and feels an enthusiasm rise within him, his pupils will feel eager, too.

"I have something interesting for you today." He produces the lava and turns it over in his hand, examining it carefully. "What do you think it is?

"A meteorite? It could be; it has holes in it like the ones we saw at the museum. It is heavy and black. But a meteorite has quite a bit of iron in it usually. How can we try to find out if this rock has a lot of iron in it?" Here the teacher pauses, produces a horseshoe magnet and an assortment of small metal objects: a penny, a silver ring, an iron nail, and a brass hook.

"Remember the lesson we had on magnets? Now, how will I know which one of these objects is iron?" He demonstrates.

"And here is a compass. If this rock contains a great deal of iron, and I move the compass closer, what will happen?" He demonstrates.

"The magnet was not attracted; the compass needle did not move. Now, what should we think?

"Feel the rock; it's heavy, isn't it? And what are all these holes in the surface? It's very irregular in shape." Pupils discuss and examine.

"If I tell you that this rock came from Hawaii, would that help?" A map, more discussion, and finally the group reaches the conclusion that the rock is lava, and that before it reached the surface of the earth it was called magma; that the holes in the rock came from escaping gases when the lava was still in a liquid state. From this point on, it is an easy step to pineapple plantations in social studies, or obsidian (volcanic glass) in science.

The chunk of lava is then put on the display table at the back of the room, together with books about related subjects such as Hawaii, pineapples, volcanoes, or possibly the destruction of Pompeii. Each one of these related materials should have been informally introduced to the class beforehand in order to stimulate interest. Pumice and heavy lava make good contrasts in studying almost any form of volcanic eruption. In fact, volcanoes offer a practical illustration of the fact that all learning is meshed to other knowledge. Here are two of the logical and intriguing steps that may confront a teacher who permits an agile-minded fifth or sixth grader to read about Pompeii:

(1) The plaster-of-Paris reconstruction of body forms during the archaeological excavation of the city is fascinating to a twelve-year-old. Such reconstruction is based on filling a mold with liquid plaster of Paris and retaining the hardened form afterwards. This makes an excellent history-science display.

(2) A group of pupils can make a volcano that will actually erupt. A conical papier-mâché model about a foot high may be built, with a four-ounce can sunk in the top to hold the ingredient of the eruption, ammonium dichromate. The volcano is put on asbestos and aluminum foil, the room is darkened, and Vesuvius is ready to erupt! The result is thoroughly satisfactory—flames, steam, smoke, and quantities of green fluffy debris pouring down. All of this learning has evolved from a chunk of lava.

A single object, well presented, can start a whole new line of thought in a classroom. This is particularly good technique for interesting the bright pupil who will do independent reading and experimentation if his curiosity is aroused. It is the job of the teacher to arouse that curiosity.

Rocks are fun. Take another kind of rock, one that contains fossils. Such a rock could be two, three, or more million years old. That fact alone is arithmetic, and can be seen in figures written on the board. If the fossil bears the imprint of a fern, remind the youngsters that years and years ago the world had great tree ferns, not unlike the mimosa trees that we have today. Or perhaps the fossil is a tribolite. Millions of years ago, tribolites ruled the world; now they are all gone.

A teacher's mind should be a compendium of fascinating trivia.

He should be able to select a suitable fact to embellish any drab lesson. Children are fascinated to learn that the dinosaurs were egg-layers (oviparous); that every single snowflake has six sides (hexagon); that a whale can drown—it is a mammal, not a fish; that the principle of the jet plane is basically the same as that of an inflated balloon which, when released, would soar in a direction opposite to the escaping air.

CHAPTER 2

Classroom Management –
Problems and Steady-Enders

Do you recall the old story about the hen and the pig gazing at a chef frying bacon and eggs?

The pig commented to the hen, "For you, this would be a contribution, but for me it would be a supreme sacrifice."

So it is when an author attempts to describe a happy, well organized classroom! The author can contribute ideas, but it is the teacher who must sacrifice strength, time, and many other interests in order to give all her talents to her pupils. She must always remember that discipleship, not coercion, is her aim. It is an art to make disciples.

Since children of the middle grades are often referred to as

"forgotten" children, we will discuss the procedures needed for good classroom management in a fourth grade. These children are forgotten because they are too old to be cute and too young to be delinquent.

Each child is the product of his home, his parents, and his grandparents. Very little can be done to alter this; it must be accepted.

Each child is the product of his previous school years from kindergarten on. Many of the child's behavior problems have already appeared in the primary grades. Very little can be done to alter this fact. Perhaps the first step in establishing discipleship is to accept the child, gifted or ungifted, and love him anyway.

The teacher brings love, patience, and a richly varied background of information to this relationship. Love must be a form of selflessness. Not "Do this because you like me" or "Do this because I want the room quiet," but "Do this because I am your teacher and we trust each other and work and learn together."

Here is a more mature approach to discipline and a more difficult one, for the teacher must not be afraid of losing dignity in gaining this permanent relationship.

Maybe the best way to begin this is with a personal confession. A good many years ago when I first started teaching, and trolley cars were still running, I had a small third-grade individualist called Mike. All one rainy Friday, he had caused me endless irritation. So, when the *final* incident occurred, I sent him to sit in the teachers' room. About five o'clock when I reached home after a long trolley ride, I remembered Mike! There was nothing to do but hurry back and worry all the way. It was still raining, but he was gone and safely home. I had *not* disciplined him. I had only removed him from my mind and my room. What had been accomplished? Would he behave better in the future? No, but I would. We must look to ourselves when the going gets rough in our classroom.

There is no substitute for a teacher with a sense of humor and the ability to make every lesson so fresh you can feel the dew on it.

Routine offers a form of security to a child; few serious discipline problems develop when a daily routine structure exists in the classroom. Should a need for control arise, there is no substitute for prompt discipline. But that discipline must not be retaliation, and it should have a personal follow-up talk for the sake of discipleship.

Many a new teacher has said, "But what do I do to discipline a child? I can't spank him. And what is more, some of them are stronger than I am!"

Discipline begins with the self-control of the teacher. When he begins to shout and threaten, and the veins stand out on his forehead, he should take time out for a moment. A long, thoughtful pause preceding a considered decision is an excellent device. An unblinking and level gaze directed at a malefactor may curb one, and a smiling shake of the head may cause another to hesitate.

If the entire class is restless, it may need a change; or perhaps the teacher himself is edgy and nervous.

When all else fails, remove the pupil from the group until he can be dealt with quietly and alone. The teacher must develop his own discipline—the principal has other things to do; he is a last resort—and discipleship is always better than coercion. A sense of humor, a clear teaching aim, and unflagging persistence are a teacher's prime assets.

Planning must be flexible and it must be versatile; and planning is organization. William Allen White once said that if three Americans fell out of an airplane, they would be organized before they reached the ground, into a president, a secretary, and a treasurer. Irrelevant as this may seem at the moment, it carries the reminder that nothing can be accomplished without careful thought beforehand. A teacher cannot afford to fumble to fill in the time; he should always have just a little more to do than he can possibly accomplish. Children need security. This is acquired when children know what is expected and have the skills with which to perform and the desire to use them. A reluctant student is a poor student. As Fritz Redl has said, "Boredom and fatigue are known to be the worst enemies of school morale."

WATCH THE STEADY-ENDER

One day, at rest time in a kindergarten, the visitor noticed a chubby, attractive little boy standing very straight and still. Suddenly from the other end of the room came a quiet little chap who began taking the medals and buttons from his chubby friend's jacket. He placed them on the teacher's desk; then both lay down on cots for a nap. When nap period was over, the quiet one went back and pinned all the medals on his friend's jacket.

Several days later, the visitor returned and saw the same procedure. "Does this happen every day?"

"Yes, I take them off and put them on—he got all those medals from cereal boxes."

In every classroom some wear the medals—others are content to pin them on. But we must watch the fellow who pins them on—sometimes he should wear them. All children need to achieve status.

On many playgrounds, you can see the negative child. She is "the steady-ender." While the others jump rope, she turns endlessly, content to see her playmates improve their jumping techniques. The steady-ender needs watching. She will never become a part of the game by remaining at the end of a rope.

The story is told of a sixth grader who always stood 'way down at the end of the baseball field and chased after balls. When asked what he had to do with the game, he replied, "I'm the wire fence." Some may say this boy received enjoyment and should be encouraged to perform this task. But where will he go from here? He, too, needs to be watched and given an opportunity to participate, not stand on the fringe of the field.

High-school teachers have been known to listen to the faltering reading of an over-age boy and say in amazement, "How on earth did you get this far, if you can't read the material?" Almost axiomatically, if the boy has trouble reading, he has equal trouble spelling, and, assuredly, a small vocabulary.

This is not hard to imagine. Many a boy (or girl) has been passed from grade to grade because he caused no trouble; because he was polite and reliable and he seemed to try. A "steady-ender" may have fairly comfortable school memories, but it is equally possible that he may never have really learned, and as the years go on, it becomes harder and harder for him to master the fundamentals. Nice, quiet students, by their very nature, may be overlooked. Paradoxically, it may handicap a child to be too "good" in school; he may receive rewards which he has not earned. In life there are neither rewards nor punishments—only consequences. If the consequence is ignorance, it is a tragedy for the child. Keep an eye on the quiet one in your class.

CHAPTER 3

Children Who Surprise Us

We are seldom able to measure children accurately. An IQ rating cannot serve as a forecast; a cultured home environment does not ensure the future; extraordinary reading ability cannot predict success; the opinion of a teacher is not a prognosis. Children are themselves, and sometimes they surprise us.

Once there was a little girl who was crippled by a deformity of the spine. She would walk behind her Quaker father when they came out of Meeting so no one would know how bent she really was. One day she asked him about the children she saw in the streets—why they seemed so ragged, dirty, and rough. He put his hand on her shoulder and replied, "My child, thee should know that there are those who have and those who have not. These have not."

So the little girl promised herself that when she grew up she would live among these people and help them, and she did just that. She moved into the middle of a slum district, and one by one invited her neighbors in to meet and know one another. As they began to know each other, they began to understand a little more, and things were better for everybody.

The little crippled girl lived to be an old lady, and when she died, people whose lives she had never touched, but who had heard and read about her, mourned the death of Jane Addams of Hull House.

Once there was a little boy whose father and mother were dead, so he lived with his grandmother. She was a little woman with big ideals. She insisted that the boy get an education so he could "grow for tomorrow." So he sold newspapers to help support the family and studied hard. When he went to the newsboys' picnic, he was not allowed to swim with them because his skin was a different

color. He won a scholarship to Harvard. He kept on "growing for to-morrow," and was awarded the Nobel Prize. He was Ralph Bunche.

Once there was a little red-haired boy with a temper who was part American and part English; he troubled his parents because he had a reading problem. Naturally, he couldn't spell either. Teachers came and went; he was a difficult pupil. Finally a teacher arrived who looked at him with different eyes; and among other things, she read him *Treasure Island*. That was the book that made him want to learn to read. Once he began to read, there was no stopping him.

We are indebted to this man for memoirs of two world wars and a life devoted to his country. As for the school teacher—when

he was in Africa, he heard that she was old and poor and very ill. So he came back to his old teacher and saw that she was taken care of during her last illness. After all, she had taught Winston Churchill to read!

Once there was another little boy whose teachers called him a bore. His parents were worried; they thought he was a retarded child. He didn't look alert and mischievous as the other boys did; he was slow and backward. It was a long time before he learned to talk, and no one thought he would ever amount to much.

By the time he was fifty years old he was world renowned, and known as a mathematical genius. Hundreds of books were written about his theory of relativity. Years before, he had been a hesitant young man fumbling for change on a streetcar. He was the great Albert Einstein.

And there was one other boy to remember; he was taught by his mother. She had sent her son to school, but was told that he apparently could not be taught. What was given him to learn one day he forgot the next, so the school dismissed him with a total of only three months' attendance. His mother became his teacher. She took him to doctors who looked at the shape of the boy's head and shook their

own sadly; the child might well have brain trouble. To this boy we owe the phonograph and the incandescent lamp. He was Thomas Edison.

Success and failure are relative words, and we cannot be quick to judge the youngsters who sit in our classrooms. Our job may well lie in understanding. Skills, facts, logical reasoning—these are the indisputable components of education. Added to these, and equally basic, is the uniqueness of the individual. Perhaps it is not so im-

portant that the teacher give of his own wisdom to the child, as it is necessary that he lead that child to the threshold of his own mind.[1]

LINCOLN AND BROTHERHOOD

In the same way, Lincoln, the popular hero, may not be just a page in history. He was an individual who has become a symbol. In

[1] Paraphrase from Kahlil Gibran, *The Prophet*. New York, Knopf, 1947, p. 64.

the struggle for racial equality he has become a symbol of hope. In the turmoil of political jealousies, he has become a symbol of statesmanship. As far as his childhood and education went, he, too, was a child who surprised us.

Let us see how this can serve us in a classroom. Imagine that you are the teacher of a fifth-grade class situated in a school where there have been much tension and several racial incidents on the playground. Your teaching requirement calls for a unit on the life and times of Abraham Lincoln; your sense of moral obligation calls for a unit on brotherhood. Inasmuch as the two seem to be compatible, you plan ahead.

You will need:

1. A map.
2. A globe.
3. Between 25 and 50 well-chosen pictures depicting Lincoln and events of his life, and also some modern photographs of monuments to make Lincoln "live" in the eyes of the students.
4. A good film or film strip on Lincoln.
5. Many easy-to-read books and some copies of old newspapers and magazines, so the class may catch the flavor of the times.
6. A collection of biographies of Lincoln.
7. One or two copies of books about George Washington Carver and his scientific works.
8. Copies of books about Ralph Bunche, Mary Bethune, Langston Hughes, and others.
9. Recordings of songs and ballads popular at that time; recordings of contemporary poetry.
10. Poetry collections with individual mimeographed copies of: "Nancy Hanks,"[2] "A Reply,"[3] "Abraham Lincoln Walks at Midnight,"[4] "The Creation."[5]

[2] Stephen V. and Rosemary Benet, "Nancy Hanks." In *Time for Poetry*. Chicago, Scott, Foresman, 1951.

[3] Julius Silberger, "A Reply to Nancy Hanks." In *Time for Poetry*. Chicago, Scott, Foresman, 1951.

[4] Gladys Adshead and Annis Duff, "Abraham Lincoln Walks at Midnight." In *An Inheritance of Poetry*. New York, Houghton Mifflin, 1948.

[5] James Weldon Johnson, "The Creation." In *God's Trombones*. New York, Viking, 1927.

These are a few of the materials which would be used to supplement materials brought in by the fifth graders themselves. The children should be encouraged to do research at home and in the local public library and museums regardless of the environment from which they come. A unit is designed to stimulate the children into reading and thinking.

Several visual (and auditory) aids can be helpful in this unit. One is a cartoon-style film strip in color entitled *Boundary Lines* which may be obtained from the B'nai B'rith Anti-defamation League of New York City. This film strip is highly recommended. It is simple, and yet so subtly profound that it carries a message right through the middle grades into adulthood; the depth of that message will be dependent upon the viewer.

Two recordings, in particular, are of interest, and duplicated scripts may be prepared to accompany them. A child needs to be prepared to see a film strip or to hear a recording. He may see or hear it many times, if it is worth while. Familiarity with words and music that are memorable is part of an education; repetition in a relaxed environment helps to build happy memories. But the first hearing or the first seeing may be strange unless the child has help. If the teacher uses a recording, he should be familiar with it himself. Music alone can be listened to, but words should be seen. Therefore, prepare and use a script, and go over the contents of that script before the recording which accompanies it is heard.

The recording called *God's Trombones* contains Negro sermons on Genesis, death, and judgment, interspersed with spirituals (Fred Waring, *God's Trombones*, Decca).

The Lonesome Train is more complicated in structure. It concerns the trip of Lincoln's funeral train from Washington, D.C., to Springfield, Ill. Abe's spirit is depicted as still living among his people; only his body is on the train. The choral singing creates the sound effects of the funeral train. A recording such as this is very worth while, but it needs explanation and vocabulary work. This can be used effectively from the middle grades through high school (Burl Ives, *The Lonesome Train*, Decca).

"The Creation," by James Weldon Johnson, is a poem that answers the age-old question, "Where did we come from?" It is

Negro in its vivid imagery, and warmly appealing in its concept of God, the Father.

The practical application of a unit on Abraham Lincoln encompasses many subjects: geography, history, reading, spelling, writing:

1. Use "Nancy Hanks," by Rosemary and Stephen V. Benet, for a discussion of questions a mother might ask.
2. Follow with "A Reply to Nancy Hanks," by Julius Silberger.
3. Using the map and globe, make a time line showing other events taking place at that time in other parts of the world.
4. If Abe Lincoln came back today, what would he say? Discuss scientific discoveries and obvious changes in today's mode of living. This will make an excellent creative writing assignment.
5. Unusual spelling words:

assassinated	lawyer	storekeeper
emancipation	slavery	honesty
proclamation	humor	union

6. Collect some Lincoln cartoons and have the class interpret them politically.
7. Learn to recite in choral speaking "O Captain, My Captain" (Walt Whitman).
8. Write items in diary as if you had been in the Civil War.
9. Learn to sing as a group "Battle Hymn of the Republic," "Tenting Tonight," "Dixie," and similar popular songs of the time.
10. What made Lincoln a great man? Here is the point where the class can think together and compile a thoughtful poem or essay.

The racial conflicts of today cannot be resolved in the schoolroom, but certainly the beginnings of intelligent understanding and brotherhood can be made there. Prejudice is an acquired vice, and must be fought against, not ignored, if men are to live together in peace.

ABRAHAM LINCOLN BIBLIOGRAPHY

BAKER, NINA BROWN. *The Story of Abraham Lincoln.* New York, Grosset & Dunlap, 1952. Upper-grade material, with ten events quickly identified through tiny illustrations on the end pages.

CAVANAH, FRANCES. *They Knew Abe Lincoln, A Boy in Indiana.* Chicago, Rand McNally, 1952. This is a charming story of Abe's boyhood from the day Dennis Hanks met his new baby cousin Abe until the Lincolns moved from Pigeon Creek.

JUDSON, CLARA INGRAM. *Abraham Lincoln, Friend of the People*. Chicago, Wilcox and Follett, 1950. The route to the White House.

KELLY, REGINA Z. *Lincoln and Douglas, the Years of Decision*. New York, Random House, 1954. The story of two great leaders in the six years prior to the Civil War.

KORAL, BELLA. *Abraham Lincoln*. New York, Random House, 1952. The illustrations in this volume tell the story of the warm, homey events in Lincoln's career. The text shows the careful editing of reading specialist Josette Frank.

LE SUEUR, MERIDEL. *Nancy Hanks of Wilderness Road, A Story of Abraham Lincoln's Mother*. New York, Knopf, 1949. This is one of the most beautiful tales about Lincoln's mother one could possibly read. It sings its memorable message so that all children will learn to love Nancy Hanks and her little baby.

MCNEER, MAY. *America's Abraham Lincoln*. Cambridge, Riverside Press, 1957. No child should go through school without having studied and enjoyed the beautiful illustrations done by Lynd Ward to accompany May McNeer's charming story.

NOLAN, JEANNETTE COVERT. *Abraham Lincoln*. New York, Messner, 1953. A well-told story of Abe from boyhood until the funeral train takes him home to Springfield.

NORMAN, GERTRUDE. *A Man Named Lincoln*. New York, Putnam, 1960. Gertrude Norman has fulfilled a great need by giving children an easy-to-read Lincoln story.

NORTH, STERLING. *Abe Lincoln, Log Cabin to White House*. New York, Random House, 1956. A fascinating story of Lincoln's stormy struggle from frontier life to the Presidency. Suitable reading for fifth and sixth grade.

PAULMIER, HILAH. *Abe Lincoln, An Anthology*. New York, Knopf, 1953. Every elementary teacher should use this anthology. In this way, children would become familiar with many anecdotes not included in their classroom texts.

BOOKS FOR BROTHERHOOD

BONTEMPS, ARNA. *Frederick Douglass: Slave—Fighter—Freeman*. New York, Knopf, 1959. The story of a slave boy who learned to read and forged his way to become a statesman and a writer.

COY, HAROLD. *The Real Book about George Washington Carver*, New

York, Garden City, 1951. When pupils read Carver's comment, "I will not be sorry for myself. That takes too much time," they will have been exposed to good, wholesome philosophy.

GOULD, JEAN. *That Dunbar Boy, The Story of America's Famous Negro Poet.* New York, Dodd, Mead, 1958. A story of struggle and success which all pre-adolescent youngsters should read and thoroughly enjoy.

GRAHAM, SHIRLEY. *The Story of Phillis Wheatley.* New York, Messner, 1949. All children will enjoy meeting a Negro girl who knew George Washington.

HUGHES, LANGSTON. *Famous American Negroes.* New York, Dodd, Mead, 1954. Brings to your classroom stories of Negroes famous in American history.

KUGELMASS, J. ALVIN. *Ralph J. Bunche, Fighter for Peace.* New York, Messner, 1952. A Negro boy who never lost pride in his race because of bitterness. His grandmother had convinced him that education and books were the most important bridges between whites and blacks.

STERNE, EMMA GELDERS. *Mary McLeod Bethune.* New York, Knopf, 1957. In a life span of 92 years, Mary McLeod Bethune saw realized her fondest dream, a school for Negro children.

CHAPTER 4

Every Teacher Is a Salesman

Recently, as we awaited our turn in a chain store, we noted this sign tacked on the side of the cash register :

You are a salesman

But remember—

When your customer gets only what he asks for—

You haven't sold a thing.

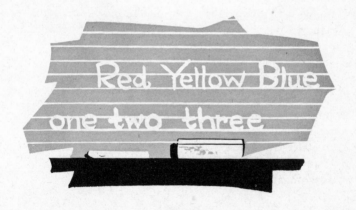

This might be just the text to use in orienting new teachers to the profession. It applies to their approach to the first day of school; it should guide them in their parent conferences and assist them in establishing good staff and community relations. Salesmanship requires preparation, a good sales talk, and keeping your customer alert to your offerings.

The first day of school your preparation will include a minute-by-minute daily schedule with all materials within reach. You will need:

> wire baskets
> all texts, music, art supplies
> games on charts, equipment if needed
> story books or anthology
> science and math equipment
> all necessary information on hand:
>> air raid rules
>> fire drill rules
>> use of lunch room
>> use of gym
>> use of auditorium

You will prepare in advance:

1. Planning *with* group on blackboard. This may seem spontaneous, but the teacher has carefully thought it out beforehand and is able to guide the group decisions.
2. A good repertoire of stories and anecdotes.
3. A few games to play in the classroom, when needed.
4. A well-written plan book, written around five steps:
   a. purpose of lesson
   b. review of material
   c. presentation of new material
   d. summary of material covered
   e. assignment of new work

Encourage primary children to suggest:

(a) "Things I wish we could do." Upper grades write lists. Some of these ideas may be impossible, but many will indicate areas you had not thought to touch upon.

(b) "Things we have done so far that I liked." Even kindergarten or first-grade children will be frank in their appraisal. The teacher must revise his plans for next week or next term with their suggestions included.

EVALUATION OF PUPILS

1. Over a period of weeks, have you seen any demonstrable changes in your pupils? Careful observation is one inexpensive and reliable form of evaluation.

2. Are records of pupils made promptly and used confidentially at parent conferences? We use the term "promptly" advisedly. If a teacher jots down a short note as soon as she observes something favorable or undesirable, she accumulates material to think about later.

One sixth-grade teacher noted that her pupils were constantly complaining about their parents. She finally suggested they write on the subject "If I Were a Parent." Here are a few actual excerpts (The first quotation comes from a boy whose father, according to local gossip, spends his weekends drinking beer and beating his wife.): "If I were a parent I would want my kids to feel proud of me. If I were a parent I would give my kids what I never had. I would try to make them grow up straight with good manners. I would want to make them feel wanted instead of dead-end kinds. That's what I'm going to do when I'm a parent."

(The second quotation comes from a boy who lives with his mother. The father has not been in evidence for some time.) "If I were a parent I would go to work and support the family. I would play with my son so that he would not lose interest in me. I would love our son very much and I would go to church with him every week."

Material such as this largely dictates its own form as it emerges. In considering the aims of a conscientious teacher, would you be willing to accept the following?

> a. In the words of Jacques Barzun ". . . she will turn a copycat into an independent thinker."
>
> b. She will hold before her group an idea, let the class view it from all sides, and then encourage them to do something about it.
>
> c. She will train the fidgety ears of her students to listen at all times.

3. Sociometric techniques may be employed where there appears to be a need for better organization within the class, but one must remember that children vacillate in their feelings, and the isolate of today may, through his own efforts, improve his situation. Or again—he may not.

It is a great help to the observant teacher to make a sociogram of her class after a few months have passed. To do this earlier would be premature because personality and scholastic adjustments must first be made before the study can be of any value. The sociogram in its simplest form is a tabulation of the interplay of personalities among your pupils. Remember that a child's first and normal desire is to be accepted by his fellows. Good grades and the approval of his teacher are secondary aspirations. Compare this thought with the old story of the missionary who went out to convert some of the starving Chinese and found that all the inspiration of his religion was as naught until he fed them. Until your child feels secure in his group, his struggle for knowledge will be only half-hearted.

What is the sociogram? A sociogram is a chart of the interrelationships within a group. Its purpose is to discover group structure . . . and the relation of any one person to the group as a whole. . . . The basic material from which a sociogram is constructed is collected from group members in answer to questions such as these: "Who are your three best friends in this group?" "What three people in this group do you most admire?"

Once a sociogram has been plotted, it is a beginning, not an end. It raises questions rather than answers them. Perhaps its greatest value is that it directs the attention to certain aspects of group structure which will lead to further observation of individual and group behavior. . . .

A sociogram is a professional instrument to be used by professional people. If it is used as a mere "popularity contest" or to reinforce a teacher's prejudice for or against certain individuals, it is better that no sociogram be made . . .

How does the sociogram help to clarify your problems? You will discover that you have a leader, a well-established circle, and a fringe group of those who have been mentioned only once. Then you find that you probably have an isolate, a child who is not accepted by the group. Need I tell you that here is your troublemaker—the pest who snatches pencils, doesn't do his homework, teases girls, gets in fights, smokes in hidden corners, and probably has a choice collection of profane words? Can you see why? He has a hidden burden; he is not accepted by his own, and he would far rather be rebuked for disorderly conduct than go unnoticed. He is usually with a group, for he cannot afford to be seen alone. As for grades, they can wait.

The well-established circle contains a group of youngsters who probably make pretty good grades and do satisfactory work. Within this group, it would seem that some correlation exists between scholarship and popularity. The fringe child appears to lie in the lower scholarship group unless he is one of the solitary souls of life who needs only a few good friends to be happy. There are some in every school. Now we come to the leader of the class, and here we find not only a popular person, but oddly enough, we may discover in some cases a lowering of academic standards. Why? Possibly in his secure and happy position the approbation of the teacher is not nearly so necessary, and being a teacher's pet can be an actual handicap. If this child is your friend, you have a real asset. If he is not your friend, you work with two strikes against you.

One more word for warning about your sociogram. Remember that it is not an answer to your problems. It merely gives you insight into the existing situation in your class. What you do with it after that depends upon your skill and your understanding of children.[1]

4. About the middle of the year the teacher will honestly ask himself, "Is my class *alive* or is it living?"

COMMUNITY RELATIONSHIPS

In the kitchen of a large cafeteria hangs this sign, "If you aren't proud of it, don't serve it." This is the motto a teacher should adopt when signing a contract. If he cannot participate in the activities because the children don't interest him, he should consider the possibility of another town that he would be proud to serve. The good teacher in a community will follow the ideal set by that great teacher Simon Patton, who was considered great because "he had one eye on the classroom and the other on the community." The pupils in our classes live in the community we serve; they like to know that we enjoy them and some of their outside activities, school-sponsored or not.

[1] From Alice M. Meeker, *I Like Children*. Reprinted by permission of Harper & Row, Publishers, Inc.

UNIT OR INTEGRATED TEACHING

A teacher may decide to work with his class on a unit plan for more than one reason: he may know that through a unit he can enhance the material presented in the course of study for his grade; children may have brought in ideas which he feels could form a background of a unit and give them an opportunity to do research.

In a carefully prepared unit the following plan is essential:

1. *Stimulate*
   a. Use actual experiences of children.
   b. See film strips and movies.
   c. Invite local people (who have traveled or written or made scientific discoveries pertinent to the unit) to speak to the class.
   d. Use newspapers, magazines, books.
   e. Read or tell a story to class.
   f. Have an exhibit of materials pertaining to the unit so children may handle them.

2. *Investigate*
   a. Make a list of questions pertaining to the unit for class to answer through reading or interviewing.
   b. Use maps, globes, charts, graphs.
   c. Take field trips.
   d. Construct things.

3. *Summarize*
   a. Be sure to summarize the information and skills acquired through integrated teaching.
   b. Teach class to outline their findings.
   c. Assemble material in scrapbooks.
   d. Use filler writing, story writing, and play writing to help with your summary.
   e. Test the results of the work in some form so that you will know the true value of the unit of work.

4. *Evaluate*
   a. What skills have been utilized and what real thinking is evidenced at conclusion of the unit?
   b. Does class show genuine understanding of all facets of the problem we have been studying?

CHAPTER 5

Every Teacher
Needs to Plan His Route

A new teacher seldom finds that he is as adaptable or as skillful as he had hoped. He is apt to find himself discouraged, overworked at times. His basic emotion seems to be a struggle for survival rather than a striving for ideals. Judson T. Shaplin expresses this succinctly when he says:

Under present conditions, much teaching is conducted under conditions of stress.

Habitual reactions or the usual defense mechanisms may be inappropriate, even crippling, under these circumstances. Practice should provide a gradual induction into teaching, a cushion against the "reality shock" which so many new teachers experience.

To illustrate the stress conditions of teaching, let me describe the rather typical experience of a beginning teacher. Common sense would suggest that his beginning load should be lighter, that it should include fewer preparations, with free periods for planning. Not at all. Given a few months' warning of his assignment, armed with a sketchy curriculum guide and an assortment of textbooks, he enters upon a full teaching schedule of five or more classes a day, and a bewildering complement of extra duties. He is treated as though he were a full-fledged, fully-certified teacher, and in theory, at least, the same expectations are held of him as for his neighbor of twenty-five years' experience. Usually his senior colleagues have chosen the favorite courses and the ablest students, so the novice quite often faces the more difficult classes of slow, bored, and belligerent students. If he has standards for himself, his work is never done—he can never know enough, plan enough, or know the feeling of completion.[1]

[1] Judson T. Shaplin, "Practice in Teaching." *Harvard Educational Review*, 31, Winter 1961, p. 35. Reprinted by permission.

Teaching is not easy, if it is done well. But if a teacher learns to anticipate the needs of himself as well as his class, he will avoid trouble. Thus he will gain confidence, *and confidence is the memory of past successes.*

Contrary to popular opinion and wishful thinking, every teacher should have planned carefully what he is going to teach and how he is going to teach it before he gets up in front of a class. In one sense, pupils are quite helpless. They must do what the teacher wants them to do, and their learning depends on his skill. If the teacher who stands before a class knows why he is doing what he is doing, then he has purpose in his teaching, and the children will sense it. An efficient teacher is a long-range planner. He would never take a trip of any distance without knowing his destination and the points along the way. Confucius has said that the best way to begin a journey of five thousand miles is to take the first step. So if the final objective is effective reading, we start with simple consonant sounds in the first grade. But each step is planned and prepared for, and made as interesting as possible along the way. The basic lesson plan includes:

Purpose
Review
Presentation (and always reading!)
Assignment

The unit is composed of many lesson plans but has a long-range purpose. The holidays are routine in that they include the basic lesson plan, but a special holiday is an oasis in teaching. It provides the theme of a new planning unit and serves as a refreshing break from routine activity. This entails careful work on the part of the teacher, for a unit is an extended period of study integrated not only into the entire day's work, but into the work of the following week as well.

But for better or worse, most teaching falls in the routine lesson category: First the larger unit, which is long-range lesson planning, and next the lesson plan, which is the guide for each subject, each day. For instance, a teacher may plan a unit on famous men. Such a unit would embrace history, reading, simple number work, geography, and language arts. It would vary in increasing complexity as the grade level rises. The lesson plan is a daily learning step within that unit.

In a formal plan book, the lesson plan may take many routine forms. Here are two outlines around which a lesson plan can be easily built:

1. *Stimulate:* (get them interested)
   Read news
   Read a story
   See a movie
   Look at pictures
   Listen to accounts of travelers
   Examine exhibits
   Tell actual experiences

2. *Investigate:* (become curious; learn study and research skills; be critical)
   Read
   Study maps, charts, globes, graphs
   Discuss
   Report
   Experiment
   Interview
   See a movie
   Take trips
   Make things
   Question

3. *Summarize:* (be sure the pupils see the meaning of the entire unit as well as its parts)
   Dramatize
   Make scrapbooks
   Write stories or letters
   Draw pictures
   Outline
   Summarize
   Test

4. *Evaluate:* (the teacher considers the result she hopes to achieve)
Social behavior
Better thinking
Skills
Understanding
Appreciations

Any daily lesson plan is built around much the same pattern for each subject taught during the day. Let us take the daily arithmetic lesson. In middle and upper grades the essential skills are taught in the morning. In lower grades periods are never longer than twenty minutes and are interspersed for variety. This will be a fifth-grade lesson, thirty minutes in length:

Subject: Arithmetic 9:00–9:30   pp. 35–36   fractions

Preparation: glass pitcher of sugar, set of glass measuring cups; single glass measuring cup

Presentation: write $1/4 + 1/4 = 1/2$ $(2/4)$. $1/2 + 1/2 = 1$ on board. Demonstrate this in theory by adding numerators of fractions which have like denominators. By reducing $2/4$ to $1/2$, $3/4$ should be larger than $2/4$. Drawing a careful analogy, demonstrate the practical truth of the theory by filling the measuring cups with sugar. $1/4$ and $1/4$ and $1/4$ should make $3/4$, and $3/4$ should be larger than $2/4$. If $2/4$ is $1/2$, then $3/4$ is more than $1/2$. Continuously correlate theory on board with practical demonstration. Permit pupils to test theory for themselves.

Review: Oral drill on reduction of fractions written on board:

8/18	8/16	4/10	6/8	2/4	6/12
4/6	3/9	18/27	14/21	3/3	6/9
10/16	4/8	6/24	8/24	9/18	2/16

Summary: Review demonstration material.

Assignment: Pass out duplicated sheets on reduction of fractions for homework; some portion of homework should include "Which is larger?" in groups of two fractions. A lesson plan similar to this should be prepared in detail for all major skills. Admittedly, this will be work. But it is necessary work, and the conscientious teacher will do it conscientiously.

SPRING AND CHRISTMAS PLANNING

Spring contains Easter and Passover, which are primarily religious holidays, but in the tax-supported public schools they take on a non-sectarian aspect that deals with the renaissance of spring. To the philosophic mind, this concept is perennial and basic.

> For there is hope of a tree if it be cut down,
> that it will sprout again,
> And that the tender branch thereof will not cease.
>
> —JOB XIV

It is the springtime that makes a young man's fancy turn to love, and makes a youngster's feet skip with joy to see the first green leaves and hear the birdcalls that he has not heard all winter long. This is Spring, and this is the theme of the unit.

First of all, the room must be made "special," and that starts with the bulletin board. In the primary grades the bulletin boards can be attractive. The children will enjoy suggesting and creating themes for the bulletin board.

Writing and spelling become integrated with art in making Easter cards for the entire family. Arithmetic becomes part of time on the calendar: the date of Easter or Passover; the first day of spring; the number of days until the bulbs on the windowsill bloom; the days of vacation and the time of return.

Storytelling time is fun. Although there are many attractive stories, the imaginative teacher will always be able to take a small situation, such as a runaway chick, and spin an original tale around it. When this is done frequently by the teacher, things begin to happen among the children. They develop the art of storytelling, too. If children have many opportunities to "build" stories, the teachers in the upper grades find composition writing a pleasure rather than a chore. Here is an example of the single familiar object and the tiny incident expanded into a satisfying story to be told to a group:

Once upon a time there was a little chick who wanted to run away. All day he had stayed beside his mother and stayed with his sisters and brothers. He was tired of being good. He stuck his little yellow head out from under his mother's wings, and peeked out through the feathers. My! The world looked exciting. It was big. It was interesting. All his little brothers and sisters were asleep; they did not think the world was exciting. All they wanted to do was sleep. He wanted to run away. So he did. He ran and ran until his little legs were tired.

Right in front of him was a big red tractor. Tiny Chick hopped onto the wheel. Then he fluttered his wings and gave a big hop—right onto the tractor seat.

He could see a lot. Tiny Chick could see the barn. He could see the silo. He could see the apple trees in blossom. But the seat of the tractor was not comfortable. It was too hot. The tractor had been sitting in the sun all day. So Tiny Chick fluttered his wings and gave a big hop—down to the ground. He ran and ran to the barn, until his frail little legs were tired.

Right in front of him was a big old sleigh that was only used in the wintertime. Tiny Chick hopped onto the runner. He fluttered his wings and gave a big hop—right onto the seat. He could see a lot. Tiny Chick could see the horse in his stall. He could see the haymow. And he could see his mother looking for him.

She was looking for Tiny Chick. "Cluck! Cluck! Come right here, young man! Where are you? Cluck! Cluck!"

Tiny Chick was not happy. He was not comfortable. The seat on the sleigh was too cold. It had been in the barn for a long time. Tiny Chick answered his mother. "Cheep! Cheep!" But she did not hear him.

"Cluck! Cluck! Where are you? Cluck! Cluck! Wait till I see you, young chick! Cluck!"

"Peep! Peep!" She could not hear him. Tiny Chick took a deep breath of air and swelled out his yellow feathers.

"Peep! Peep! PEEEPP!" And he fluttered his wings and gave a BIG jump. And he ran to his mother until his little legs were tired.

She was very glad to see him. She clucked and smoothed him with her bill. It was getting dark and the air was getting cool. It was time to have some supper and go to bed. Tiny Chick snuggled under his mother's feathers. It was warm. It felt good. In fact, it felt just right.[2]

Jokes and stories relax the nervous tensions of a classroom in the same way that games relax the restless bodies of children. Every teacher should have a variety of games in his repertoire. Here is an

[2] An original story by the author.

example of one which has different names for different months. It is as adaptable as a quart of milk, and just as suitable for any age!

Choose two teams: For example, with twenty-nine children, fourteen may be bluebirds, and fourteen robins. One child is the bird-catcher who stands in the middle of the room and calls, "Bluebirds, fly!" and all the bluebirds dash from one end of the room to the other. Any children caught by the bird-catcher must go to the left side of the room and stand in the "birdcage."

Adaptations are easy:

	Teams	Catcher	Penalty
September	squirrels and chipmunks	game warden	the oak tree
October	witches and goblins	ghost	the graveyard
November	turkeys and Pilgrims	Indian	Massachusetts
December	toy soldiers, dancing dolls	Santa Claus	Santa's workshop
January	blizzards and snow flurries	Jack Frost	North Pole
February	Valentines and Cupids	mailman	post office
March	Murphys and Kellys	leprechaun	Ireland
April	bluebirds and robins	bird catcher	birdcage
May	sailboats and motorboats	captain	dry dock

Young children love to repeat the catchy little jingles about Marshmallow, a rabbit whose true story appears in a book by Clare Newberry. Later the jingle may be used on charts as part of the bulletin board and then copied on individual papers and illustrated:

> A bunny is a quiet pet
> A bunny is the best thing yet.[3]

Christmas, like Easter, is primarily a religious holiday. It has weeks of preparation and commercialized carols; the excitement seeps into the classroom. No teacher can fight it, so join it—but it may not be religious, in the public schools.

Parties, gifts, songs, and stories are the order of the day. Parties will be held throughout the school as a matter of course; gifts are part of the gaiety; songs are traditional; but good stories are hard to come by, and nobody needs a good Christmas story more than a primary teacher:

[3] Clare T. Newberry, *Marshmallow*. New York, Harper, 1942.

When Santa Claus Changed His Suit

One night Santa Claus was just putting the last toys in his sled and went back to the workshop to get a doll he had forgotten, when he heard a little voice. The voice came out of the corner of Santa Claus's workshop. It said, "Say, Santa Claus, aren't you tired of your old red suit?"

When Santa Claus turned around he saw a mouse, but it wasn't the kind of a mouse you children are used to seeing. The little mouse said, "Look what I did! I got tired of my old gray velvet suit, so I put a piece of red ribbon around me and I stuck a darning needle in it for a sword and I found a silver thimble and I put it on my head for a hat. Don't you think I look better, Santa Claus?"

Santa Claus said, "You look very nice, little mouse."

"Well, why don't you change your suit, Santa Claus? We're all awfully tired of your old red suit," said the little mouse.

Santa Claus got into his sled and as he rode along the road he said, "Maybe the little mouse is right. I have been wearing this red suit for a long time, perhaps I should change my suit."

So Santa Claus pulled his sled off the road into the woods and he got out a big box, and in the box was an overcoat that he was taking to Farmer Jones, and a nice new gray fedora hat. Santa Claus pulled off his old red suit; he put on the overcoat, tucked his beard inside, buttoned the overcoat over his beard, and put on the fedora hat. As he went in the front door, a little boy who should have been in bed, but wasn't, peeked down over the stairway and he said, "Mother! Daddy! Hurry up, come downstairs, there's a burglar coming in the front door."

So Santa Claus dropped a bag of toys for the children and ran back to the sled. As he rode down the street, he said, "I don't think I should wear Farmer Jones's overcoat," and he took it off and put it back very carefully in the box and he put the nice felt fedora hat back in the hatbox. He said, "Maybe I would look better in an Indian suit. I have a nice Indian suit I bought for a boy down the street."

So Santa Claus put on the Indian suit and he put on a beautiful feather headdress and he tucked his beard inside the Indian suit and he said, "Well, I won't go down the chimney here because I don't want to get soot in my feathers." So he put one foot in the front window and he dropped a bag of toys in the window.

But before he had a chance to pull his other foot in, a little girl who should have been in bed, but wasn't, peeked down the stairs and said,

"Mother! Daddy! Hurry up quick! There is an Indian in the living room!"

Santa Claus had to jump out the window, jump into his sled and ride down the road as fast as he could away from the house. Then he said, "I don't think I look well in an Indian suit." So he took off the Indian suit and he put it very carefully back in the box for the boy down the street.

He tucked the feathers in the box and then he said, "I know what I'll do. I have a fireman's uniform with a nice shiny badge. I'll try the fireman's uniform."

So he put on the fireman's uniform and he polished up the brass badge and he put it on his coat. Then he put on the peaked hat, took a bag of toys for the children and walked down the street. He opened a window and stepped in and was just putting the toys under the tree when a little boy, who should have been in bed, but wasn't, peeked over the banister and said, "Mother! Daddy! Hurry up quick, the house is on fire." Santa had just enough time to jump back in the sled and go down the street a little way. He said, "I don't think I look well in a fireman's uniform. After all, I don't think there is anything as becoming to Santa Claus as his old red suit."

So he took off the nice shiny badge and the fireman's uniform and fireman's hat and packed them all in the box for the little boy down the street. He pulled his beard out over his red suit and he put on his red hat, and from that day to this Santa Claus has always worn his old red suit.

—ANONYMOUS

OVERCOMING MONOTONY IN READING

The first-grade teacher needs a change now and then. The material he has used seems monotonous, and he feels a yearning for something really new for his boys and girls. He has forgotten his own ingenuity. He can make his own new primer, illustrate it with stick figures, and duplicate it. A paper cutter and a stapler will make it into a usable child's book to be read, colored, or done with as he wishes. Duplicating forty will be no more trouble than duplicating ten. Each page should have just a few sentences, and plenty of white around the border. Two pages to the stencil, which is then cut in half, make an excellent page size.

Chicken Hotel

1   Tim was going to see his grandmother.
His mother took him to the bus.
"Get out at the old hotel," she said.

2   Tim climbed on the bus.
He put in his money.
He sat by the window.

3   The bus hummed along.
It passed the church.
It passed the school.
It passed the candy store.

4   Soon the bus was in the country.
Tim had fun counting the farmhouses.
The first one was big.
The second one was middle-sized.
The third one was little.

5   By and by Tim saw the hotel.
He rang the bell and the bus stopped.
Just then he saw something.
"What a surprise!" shouted Tim.

6   Every Saturday, Tim saw the old hotel.
Every Saturday, he saw boards on all the windows.
Now, the windows were open.

7   Tim ran over to see what had happened.
"What funny screens," he said.
"They are made of chicken wire."

8   Just then, Tim had another surprise.
Chickens came to the bedroom windows and looked out at Tim.
He looked in the living room.
He saw chickens on the table.

9   He looked in the kitchen and saw chickens on the old stove.

10   Tim went around to the porch.
     He laughed and laughed and laughed.
     There sat a rooster in an old rocking chair.
     There sat a hen in an old rocking chair.
     They were taking sun baths.

11   Tim went down the street to Grandmother's house.
     "Grandmother, have you seen the chicken hotel?" said Tim.
     "No," said Grandmother, "but I want to buy eggs. Let us go
     to the farm."

12   "I like your chicken hotel," said Tim.
     "Thank you," said the farmer. "That is a good name. I will
     put it on a sign."

13   Now, when the bus stops you can see this sign:
          CHICKEN HOTEL
          EGGS FOR SALE
          GET READY FOR EASTER (This last line is optional.)[4]

An average first-grade class will be able to read a book like this
after a few months of instruction. Since basic readers never go
home, material such as this will enable the child to read to his parents and add a book to his own "library."

SPRING BIBLIOGRAPHY

BROWN, MARGARET WISE. *The Golden Bunny*. New York, Simon and
     Schuster, 1953. A charming collection of stories, poems, and best
     of all, an alphabet for a hungry bunny. Suitable for nursery–
     primary children.
FENNER, PHYLLIS R. (comp.) *Feasts and Frolics*. New York, Knopf,
     1950. A good collection of stories for every holiday, especially good
     for middle grades.
HARPER, WILHELMINA (comp.). *Easter Chimes—Stories for Easter and
     the Spring Season*. New York, Dutton, 1942. All lovers of fine ma-
     terial for children will enjoy using this collection of stories, poems,
     and folk tales.

[4] Original story by the author.

KONKLE, JANET. *Easter Kitten*. Chicago, Children's Press, 1955. This time an attractive kitten helped the Easter Rabbit fill the baskets for the children.

LEONARD, RACHEL. *Mrs. Roo and the Bunnies*. Boston, Houghton Mifflin, 1953. A humorous tale of a kangaroo offering taxi services for bunnies.

McCREADY, T. L., JR. *Increase Rabbit*. New York, Ariel Books, 1958. A story written for third or fourth graders with beautiful, detailed illustrations.

MILHOUS, KATHERINE. *The Egg Tree*. New York, Scribner's, 1950. Just the right book to encourage budding artists in the upper grades to create their own designs for decorating eggs. Also a good introduction to Pennsylvania Dutch customs.

RATHBUN, HELEN KELLEHER. *Easter Surprise*. New York, Crowell, 1947. An entertaining story for any child who invests 50¢ and has to wait for results.

STEINER, CHARLOTTE. *My Bunny Feels Soft*. New York, Knopf, 1958. An excellent book for a preschool child, dramatizing the excitement of "touch" in sparkling colors and verse.

WILLIAMS, GARTH. *The Rabbits' Wedding*. New York, Harper, 1958. The rabbits' wedding gives children a good feeling—black rabbits and white rabbits can be wondrously happy together.

ZOLOTOW, CHARLOTTE. *The Bunny Who Found Easter*. Berkeley, Parnassus Press, 1959. The search of the lonely bunny for Easter gives a child a brief look at each season and its characteristics.

CHAPTER 6

You Can Be a Creative Teacher

Creative writing never takes the place of disciplined writing; it is a supplement, and it serves the needs of the individual child. Proper procedure and drill are uniform for all, but imagination and ideas are very private and very precious to the single person. That's why authors write books—to express their own thoughts—and what pleasure to see these thoughts in print!

To use another analogy: the words "every child" and "each child" are used almost interchangeably, but there is a subtle difference. Disciplined writing is like *every* child: all must learn. Creative writing is like *each* child: an individual has written it.

And this is important, for ever since John Dewey, the philosophy of the American schools has been "to give to each the opportunity to become that which he is capable of becoming." Individuality is the hidden flower of the conformative classroom.

Creativity is so basic that even the weakest reader can read what he himself has written. Here is one door to learning that is always open. Many a child, facing the hurdles of spelling, vocabulary, sentence structure, and groping thought, is very nearly inarticulate. For him, creative writing is more painful and more necessary than it would be for another. Writing is communication. Creative writing, in grammar school, is a sort of spontaneous communication, and prepares the youngster for later and more rigorous training in the use of words.

In practical application, a good teacher first strives to stimulate the imagination. He can have no idea of the precise catalyst that will

perform that miracle, so he provides many opportunities. He may, for instance, place a table in front of the class, and on the table put:

a red neckerchief
a popular magazine with a picture of an astronaut on the cover

a wax pumpkin
a bottle of perfume
a piece of fur
a key
a tuning fork
several coins
a stuffed owl
a black boot
an old tennis shoe
three or four dolls
and a variety of similar articles.

He covers the entire collection with a long mysterious black velvet evening cape. All this preparation has been done before class, so when the pupils come in, they are almost immediately interested. This helps. He explains that under the cloak there will be many interesting things. They will discuss these articles, look at them, and handle them, even take them back to the desks to examine if necessary. But each pupil will write a story about the object he chooses. No hurry. Yes, he will be glad to answer any questions, to help with any spelling problems. Everyone who writes a story will be an author, and all authors will please put their names on the covers of their stories.

So he and the class discuss what they see on the table. The children run their hands over the objects and examine them thoroughly. One by one they begin to write.

This served as an actual demonstration lesson with a heterogeneous grouping of youngsters from fourth and fifth grade, with these results:

I'd like to go to the moon. I think it would be exciting because I could do just about everything on the moon. By the way would you like to go to the moon? Well if you did you could pick up heavy rocks and many other things like equipment. It is very funny on the moon because you would not be able to make a hole in your shirt like some people do when they play. Why! because if you tear a hole in your shirt all the air in your shirt or pants would come out. And you could die as quickly as you could on earth. If I had an expedition I would be very proud.

I think this riding boot has been in the cuff of a horse. I think the man who wore this black riding boot must have fallen off the horse once or twice.

This boot was not used for walking much because it is not scuffed up badly.

This boot is old because it is worn out in the inside of the shoe, and the soul is off at the bottom of the shoe.

This coin is a half dollar. It was made 1893 and is 68 years old. The man on the coin is Calumbus and on the bake of coin Calumbus ship.

Once there was an owl named Too Too. He was a small, young and curious.
One day Too Too was walking through some woods looking for mice and other rodents (rodents are small animals about the size of a mouse). All of a sudden he heard a dog barking. So instead of going away from the sounds, he went towad the sound. Finalle he found a clearing in some Oak trees. There were some children picnicing in the clearing. There by the edge of the clearing was a big boy teasing a dog. Two small children trying to make him stop teasing the dog. But the big bully wouldn't stop teasing the dog. So the two children jumped on him with fists and feet which surprised the boy very much. The dog ran away and the children got of the boy and let him alone.

A week ago we used tuning forks to make sound. The tuning forks wher set on a wooden table, then we hit the tuning on the table and we proved that sound is vibrating air.

Once in school we took a piece of paper and put it in a glass, then we put the glass in water and five minutes we took the glass out and the paper was not wet.

Nothing interesting ever happens thought Helen. And theres never anything to do. I think I'll play dolls theres nothing else to do. So she went in the attic to find one of her old dolls.

Ow! She fell over a box. She looked down at ther feet and saw a rusty old key. I wonder where this came from? she said wonderingly. But she put it in her pocket anyway. As she walked along in the attic she silently thought about the key. She turned her head and thought she saw a small door knob. She walked over to it and twisted it. It opened into a tiny room.

A long time ago a large cent was only worth a cent. Now a large cent is worth over 10 times as much. A large cent is from 1850 is over 1 century old. A large cent is twice as big. I now four different kinds of pennys. They are: large cent, indian head cent, lincoln memorial cent. The large cent was made in 1850.

All of this is original work, obviously. Its spontaneity is so readily apparent that the reader can make a fairly accurate guess as to the sex of the child, his personality, and his natural acumen. Samples of creative work such as these are completely charming. But charm is not enough. As Da Vinci said, "The greatest tragedy is when theory outstrips performance."

When a fourth grader starts to write about an owl and completely leaves the bird fifty words later to end up with "The dog ran away and the children got of the boy and let him alone," the result may seem childlike and appealing. But if this same youngster writes much the same way, on a different topic, in high school, the result is appalling. The foundations for correct writing and spelling are gently but firmly laid in the grammar-school years.

First, a boy or girl should have an idea and write freely about it. *Then he learns to proofread and correct his own work with help as needed.* Then, and this is drill but very necessary, his work is ready for the bulletin board or the display table for parents to see. Creative writing is free, but within a disciplined atmosphere.

A creative teacher is a versatile and ingenious teacher, but a flexible one with a sense of humor. The class will be a reflection of that leadership.

Creative writing takes many forms. Here is an essay written by a child of ten on a bird and a beast:

The bird that I am going to write about is the Owl. The Owl cannot see at all by day and at night is as blind as a bat.

I do not know much about the Owl, so I will go on to the beast which I am going to choose. It is the Cow. The Cow is a mammal. It has six sides, right, left, and upper and below. At the back it has a tail on which hangs a brush. With this it sends the flies away so that they do not fall into the milk. The head is for the purpose of growing horns and so that the mouth can be somewhere. The horns are to butt with, and the mouth is to moo with. Under the cow hangs the milk. It is arranged for milking. When people milk, the milk and there is never an end to the supply. How the cow does it I have not yet realised, but it makes more and more. The cow has a fine sense of smell; one can smell it far away. This is the reason for the fresh air in the country.

The man cow is called an ox. It is not a mammal. The cow does not each much, but what it eats it eats twice, so that it gets enough. When it is hungry it moos, and when it says nothing it is because its inside is all full up with grass.[1]

Original writing such as this makes hilarious reading for adults, and it has given the child practice in spelling and self-expression. But more than that—it has a built-in appeal for all conscientious teachers: after reading this, one knows exactly why field trips are important!

IF YOU HAVE CHILDREN WITH A LANGUAGE PROBLEM

Years ago, many magazines carried an ad for a correspondence course in piano. The picture showed a man playing the piano, his family enthralled listening to his accomplishment. Above the picture was the caption, "To think I can play Beethoven after six lessons."

A teacher's workshop does not guarantee to solve all your problems but it does help any teacher, particularly a new teacher, to find solutions to some of the difficulties.

Suppose you were teaching in a neighborhood where most of the children had recently arrived from an entirely different life—and moved into the local school district and into your classroom. Because so many children of Puerto Rican Spanish-speaking parents have become part of our school population, we will consider a work-

[1] Reprinted with permission of Alfred A. Knopf, Inc., from *Plain Words: Their ABC* by Sir Ernest Gowers. Copyright 1954 by Alfred A. Knopf, Inc.

shop on introducing Puerto Rican customs to our teachers and American customs to our children. Here are some practical suggestions:

1. Secure an assembly room large enough to exhibit crafts and handiwork from Puerto Rico.

2. Secure a Puerto Rican teacher who has recently arrived in your city but speaks English fluently.

3. Invite a social worker and a clergyman from the neighborhood to meet with you.

4. Don't try to cover too much material, but find out from the teacher the basic vocabulary you must develop to have any real learning going on in your classroom. This will involve action words, family words, items of clothing and a few other picture words or nouns.

5. Try to have chart paper available so that all teachers, regardless of grade level, may during some part of the day actually make picture charts with Spanish-English words next to the pictures.

6. Secure a few teachers who can draw simple or stick figures to make scenes involving action such as going to the lunchroom, going to the bathroom, going to church, going to the park; label these charts, too.

7. Find out from the social worker how you can arrange to see mother or father at a time when someone will help interpret your conference.

8. Learn a few songs so that children will know you are interested in their homeland.

9. Ask the priest or minister if he can suggest a few books that you may read to understand these people better.

10. Request help from your local librarian. She will look up and secure easy reading books for these parents and their children.

11. Both pastor and social worker will be able to identify one or two capable people in your school district who will come and inform you on holiday customs, so dear to these children.

12. Plan your next workshop around these customs; draw up outlines of legends, books, music, food, crafts, pertinent to the holidays.

13. Most important—draw in the parents through a movie or some type of entertainment which will encourage them to come to the school building. A list of films available should be compiled at this workshop.

14. Encourage the children in fifth and sixth grades to tell you all they can remember about Puerto Rico and be sure to utilize it in your discussion, art, reading, spelling, and games.

15. Be sure that careful records of workshops, materials, and sources are duplicated and given to all teachers who attend.

16. Have frequent "Sharing Workshops" to which a few parents may be invited so that your influence extends beyond the school day.

A form on which the workshop can be evaluated will guide you in planning your succeeding ones. Every teacher anxious to grow in the profession will volunteer to assist with or set up a curriculum workshop. Here evaluation is essential.

Work Shop Evaluation Sheet

1. How well did the total program meet your expectations? (Check on scale below.)

Very well	Fairly well	Somewhat	To a slight degree	Not at all

2. As you review the program for the day, did any one part stand out in your estimation as being of particular value to you? _____ If your answer is yes, which part?

3. What questions did you have that are still unanswered? Would you like to pursue them further next year?

4. The program committee will appreciate any suggestions you care to give for the planning of the next meeting.

Thank you. (Use back of page for additional comments.)

CHAPTER 7

You Can't Do Business with an Empty Wagon

Years and years ago, our kitchen wall held a calendar on which we kept all our family memos. The notations have long since vanished, but the calendar picture seems as vivid as ever: An old wagon was drawn by a horse wearing a straw hat; the sides of the cart were thick with household utensils and the tailboard sagged with pails and mops; cooking pots swung on hooks underneath. Merchandise so overflowed the vehicle that the peddler was forced to lead his horse, and they trudged the road together.

Across the top of the picture ran the caption: *You can't do business with an empty wagon!*

In the same way, a teacher cannot effectively instruct a class unless he is fully equipped with plans, methods, an abundance of materials, and workable ideas. The peddler and the teacher are both salesmen; each needs a stock in trade.

The difference between a capable teacher and an exceptional one lies not so much in education and techniques as in this repertoire of ideas that enables routine material to be supplemented in a variety of ways.

The work of the hands should supplement the work of the head. It is almost axiomatic that children learn at different rates and in different ways. Like the peddler's wagon, the teacher's mind should be filled with many ideas. He should be able to take inexpensive materials and transform them through imagination and handicraft into a tangible extension of their regular classroom procedures. Teaching need never be dull if it is spiced with ingenuity.

59

"Trash or Treasure" is a collection of practical ideas for all grades, requiring only inexpensive materials and a minimum of explanation. Aside from the practical value of a list of ideas adaptable to many grades and many occasions, this collection serves the teacher in other ways:

1. Too many parents are apt to judge the quality of their child's elementary school education by the work he brings home. This is a form of public relations that the teacher should accept. Mother's Day, Christmas or Hanukkah, Thanksgiving, Hallowe'en, Easter—all of these are times in which a primary-grade child will bring tangible evidence of his classroom work to his parents.

2. "Art work" is a euphemistic expression for room decoration, bulletin-board displays, and busy work. This is not entirely bad; neither is it entirely good. A room should be decorated with children's work—it's their room—and bulletin boards should be changed frequently. There even comes a time when Johnny needs the calming influence of simple directions, paint, glue,

scissors, and colored paper so the rest of the class may work in peace. If handicraft is used as a substitute for real teaching, it is not good, of course.

3. Even if a class of thirty makes thirty Thanksgiving turkeys, much can be learned. No two of those turkeys will be identical, and each child will have acquired a lesson in following directions. Creative art is highly desirable, but learning to follow instructions is equally essential.

4. Maps, puppets, papier-mâché models to enrich textbook material in the upper grades are invaluable teaching aids. Many a child learns better if his hands supplement his book learning.

The flannel-board and yarn-ball directions are indispensable teaching aids in the elementary school. The yarn ball is the soft ball for indoor games, and the perfect colorful gift made by the upper grades for small children. The flannel board has unlimited teaching potential, and will reflect the teacher's own resourcefulness.

TRASH OR TREASURE

Door Knocker

This door knocker is made by inserting a piece of coarse twine, about 12 inches long, through two empty spools and then tying a knot in the twine. The child can color or paint the spools and write his name on them. The knocker may be fastened to his bedroom door by running a tack through the twine just above the knot and driving it into the door. Thus he has a name plate as well as a knocker on his door.

Spool Lamp

Bend a piece of pipe cleaner, about 6 inches long, in half. Run one end of the doubled pipe cleaner through an empty spool and the other end through a paper candy cup. Draw designs on the spool if wanted, then twist another piece of pipe cleaner around the bottom.

Doll Bassinet

Fasten top and bottom of a box together with cellophane tape and paste a ribbon bow and lace ruffle (cut from a paper doily) to the box. Make a rattle by running a threaded needle through a few grapefruit seeds, then loop through the end of the box.

Pincushion

Materials used: tuna-fish can, 3 old socks, and construction paper. Stuff 2 socks in washed can and save third for covering can. Scallop a piece of the paper to fit around can. Ribbon might be used to hold paper.

Santa Claus

Materials used: apple, marshmallows, and Christmas seal. Fasten marshmallows onto apple with toothpicks to form arms and legs. Place seal on one marshmallow and fasten to top of apple for head.

Flowerpots

Made from condensed-milk cans painted with quick-drying enamel. Could be used in classroom for growing seeds or as a gift for Mother.

Fan

Materials used: construction paper, lace doily, and ribbon. Paste doily on paper and fold like accordion. Cut edge from another doily and paste around edge of fan. Cut construction paper to fit lace edge. Bring folds together at bottom and fasten with ribbon.

Thanksgiving Turkey

Made from potato with toothpicks for legs and tail and head from construction paper inserted in slits made in potato.

Paper Weight

Made from stone painted.

KNITTING BOX

Made from oatmeal box covered with wallpaper or finger-painted paper. Braid yarn and fasten to box for handle.

PLAQUES

Grease saucer; mix plaster of Paris; place design on plate; pour plaster into saucer; place fastener in saucer for a wall hook before plaster hardens. When hardened slide from saucer.

VASE

Use empty glass jar of desired size. Paint with quick-drying enamel for design.

PLASTER PINS

Mix plaster of Paris; pour into a small mold; place safety pin in plaster before it hardens; remove from mold; paint.

SNOWBALLS OR FLOWERS

Cut tissue paper into 30 pieces, about 3″ by 4″. Fold each piece diagonally twice and thread the resulting triangle at the apex on a piece of green yarn or twine 4″ long. Press all the triangles together in the center of the string. Trim edges if desired.

PAPIER-MÂCHÉ MAP

1. Get road map from any service station.
2. Cover back of map with dark pencil or crayon.
3. Fasten map on board.
4. Trace outline of map—imprint of pencil will outline map on board.
5. Place papier-mâché within outline.
6. Papier-mâché can be molded to any shape desired.

To Make Papier-Mâché

1. Take any old newspapers and tear into small pieces.
2. Place these pieces into pail half full of water.
3. Let soak for a few days.
4. If you want the mâché quickly have the children "mash" it for an hour.
5. Papier-mâché will harden after being pressed into place.
6. Use no glue or flour.

Papier-Mâché Figure

Materials used: newspaper, printed and plain, two wires from spiral notebooks, wallpaper paste, tempera paint, odds and ends for clothing, yarn for hair, sequins for eyes.

Directions: Bend wire; form loop at top of head. Bend bottom for legs. If feet are desired, fasten metal discs to bottom a bit smaller than final size. Take second wire and fasten for shoulders and arms. Make loop at each end for hands. Fill in wire and form shape with crushed newspaper. Tie in place. Put layer of papier-mâché on top of this. Let dry. Do this three times, the third time using plain news. Smooth. Make features. Cover with a layer of plain news. Let dry. Paint. Paste features on, such as sequin eyes and yarn hair. Add clothes. (Shellac figure if desired.)

INDIAN HEADDRESS

Band made from colored pages from magazine, pieces cut 5" × 3" and folded lengthwise twice—ends folded toward middle. Slip one into the other, weaving fashion. Real feathers may be used and stuck into slits in weaving.

EASTER PARTY FAVOR

Use sandwich bag to hold candy. Head and neck are made from cardboard taken from man's laundered shirt and stapled onto back of bag on inside. Feet are stapled also. Head and feet may be made in the form of rabbit or duck. Tie with ribbon at neck.

SHELL BIRD

Body and head are made from shells. Neck and legs are pipe cleaners. Glue onto a small piece of cardboard to make it stand.

CHRISTMAS BELLS

Cover paper cups with red crepe paper. Use pipe cleaners for stem of clapper. Form clapper with cotton and cover with crepe paper. Fasten bunch together with red crepe-paper bow.

MAILBOX

Made with two rectangular cardboard meat plates. Put a slot in one of the containers to receive the letters. Paint the box or use crayons to cover the box. Use designs if you wish them. Sew the two parts together on the left side.

INDIAN HEAD

Made with salt box covered with brown paper. Draw or paint the face. Use a piece of cloth for hair. Wind black thread around cloth to form braids. Draw bright colored beads around Indian's neck. Cut a feather headdress from oak tag. Color feathers many colors. Attach feathers.

TAMBOURINE

Made with two paper pie plates. Place a design on backs of plates. Shellac the plates. Put pebbles or pieces of metal in plates and sew together. Remove corks from pop bottle tops and fasten to edges. Add crepe-paper streamers.

APPLE BANK

Made from papier-mâché over an apple. Put paste all over the apple skin. Then cover with newspaper strips which have been dipped in water. Continue doing this until it is the thickness you desire. Allow it to dry, then cut in half to remove the apple. Paste together again. Make a slit for money. Paint or use nail polish to color.

CLOWN BEANBAG

Make the head and fill with beans. Make a gathered neck. Sew up two pieces of material for legs. Attach yarn feet.

DECORATIVE CONTAINER

Use for buttons, nails, screws, or odds and ends. Paint coffee can. Make a hole for knob handle. Put on decals or designs from construction paper.

PENNY BANK

Made from jar with metal top. Make slit for coins. Paint with nail polish or paint. Decorate with decals.

DOORMAT

Made from board 12″ × 18″ with used bottle caps nailed to board (about 15¢).

RHYTHM INSTRUMENT (RATTLE)

Made from small metal box with wood for handle. Place several pieces of wood or pebbles inside box. Enamel with Chinese red paint.

BRACELET

Made from shell macaroni. Enamel various colors. Make holes by using nail and inserting into shells. String with elastic thread.

POMANDER

Made from orange or apple stuck full of cloves. Wrap in newspaper and keep in warm dry place for two weeks or until completely dehydrated. Put ribbon around in several different directions and leave loop for hanging.

TRINKET BOX

Made from plastic cheese container painted with forest-green enamel. Use head of wooden clothespin for knob.

SANTA CLAUS

Made from red and white construction paper. Face is white circle, body is red circle, hat is red triangle. Arms and legs are strips of red 1″ × 18″ folded and fastened on body with staples. Cotton may be used for trimming on hat, beard, and buttons on suit.

BUNNY FACE

Made from oak tag with rabbit features crayoned. Whiskers made from pipe cleaners. Cut holes for eyes. Paint inside of pop-bottle caps with white paint. Place small colored buttons in bottle caps and place in cellophane over scotch tape. Make box from crepe paper fastened under chin with staples.

WALL PLAQUE

Child presses hand into a flattened lump of soft clay. Press pencil through top for hole to hang by.

FINGER PUPPETS

Make small paper dolls without legs. Fasten to fingers with rubber bands, using fingers for dolls' legs.

CLAY HEARTS

Use soft clay, smoothly flattened. Cut out heart with cookie cutter. When thoroughly dry, paint and shellac.

DOORSTOP

Made from clay into shape of dog's head, painted and shellacked.

CLOTHES SPRINKLER

Made from catsup bottle painted and decorated with decal. Top can be bought in 5 and 10.

SMALL PICTURES FOR CHRISTMAS GIFTS

Made from vacuum canning lids. Cut pictures from magazines or old Christmas cards (small snapshots are nice to send to Grandma). Glue a bit of ribbon in a loop to hang picture.

KLEENEX FLOWER

Fold 2 facial tissues lengthwise. Cut down the middle with pinking shears. Trim remainder of tissue with pinking shears. Fold in half and fasten with a wire to use for stem. Spread out folds of tissue by opening. Wind green tissue around wire for stem. Make appropriate leaves for flower from crepe paper or construction paper.

WASTEBASKET

Made from ice cream container (gallon size). Paint with enamel. Apply design.

NECKLACE

Made from dried watermelon seeds and colored dried cantaloupe seeds. String with needle and thread and tie with ribbon.

MITTEN PIN-AND-NEEDLE CASE

Cut two mittens from red felt or flannel, add several thicknesses of white flannel same size as red. Tie together at wrist.

BANK

Made from pint size ice-cream carton. Paste on round piece of white cardboard. Decorate like Uncle Sam's hat. Cut slit in top for coins.

PARTY FAVOR

Made from discarded cardboard tube covered with crepe paper and fastened with sticker. Fringe ends and tie with ribbon. Candy may be placed inside.

DOORSTOP

Made from fieldstone painted with flat paint. Design painted with oil paints. Shellac. Felt may be pasted on bottom to prevent scratching.

PARTY BASKET

Made from pint size ice-cream carton covered with crepe paper. Decorate with appropriate stickers or pictures cut from seed catalogs. Handle is made from strip of oak tag.

LITTLE RED HEN HOOD

Made from paper bag large enough for child's head. Fold at top and paste in red comb made from construction paper. Cut up folds on side to form beak. Paint beak yellow and eyes yellow with black pupil. Run string through bottom for drawstring.

PEEP-IN EASTER EGG

Made from cardboard tube which once held paper ribbon. Paint inside of tube like sky and grass. Glue small rabbit so he looks as though he is sitting in grass. Pad tube with crushed newspaper and tie with string forming something that resembles an egg. Paste piece of tissue paper at one end of tube. Cover newspaper with papier-mâché. Decorate with tempera colors.

EASTER BUNNY

Made from empty spool covered with cotton. Cut bunny head and crayon features. Paste on one end of spool and on other end of spool paste bunch of cotton.

BOATS

Carve boats from balsa wood. Use paper for sails. These might be used for Columbus Day or a science lesson.

Columbus' Boats

Made from walnut shells with melted wax poured into upturned shells to hold toothpick masts. Sails made from paper.

Clock Face

Made from paper plate inverted. Numbers might be cut from old calendar. Hands are made from black paper fastened in middle of plate with paper fastener.

Totem Pole

Made with assorted boxes pasted one on top of the other. Wings are made with oak tag and slipped through slits in boxes. Designs are painted with tempera.

Finger Play Puppets

Use white paper that has been folded and pasted so it can be slipped on finger. Draw pictures of five little pigs or any five animals desired and use as finger puppets.

Coasters

Made from jar lids. Paint with either aluminum paint or black enamel and place decal in center of inside. Coasters may also be made from old drainboard cover (rubber).

Magnet Doll

Cut out shape of boy doll from old felt hat. Place magnet between two pieces cut for legs and sew them together.

Christmas Card

Made from 9″ × 12″ red paper folded in four. Inside message cut from old card. Sprig of evergreen painted in water color on white paper pasted on outside of card. Real pine cones pasted on sprig of evergreen.

Spool Doll

Materials: two spools and 6 pipe cleaners. Put 4 pipe cleaners through both spools for feet. Twist. To make the arms lay a cleaner across in front of the spool and another across the back of it just under the upper rim. Twist the cleaners together to make arms.

STOCKINET DOLL

Materials: one sock, rags for stuffing, embroidery cotton. Cut one half of foot away to make arms. Remainder of foot makes feet. Tie at top for hat. Embroider on features.

MR. BUBBLENOSE

Made from old sock. Cut away sock just below heel. Make nose by stuffing the toe with tissue paper and fasten it in place by winding a rubber band around it. Sew on two buttons for eyes. The head is stuffed with more tissue paper and the body with old rags or cotton. Sew open end of sock and tie a bright ribbon around the neck.

PUPPET

Head made from small match box or one of comparable size. Odds and ends are used for clothing, which is sewn or pasted to box. Make frill around neck to cover joining. Yarn or roving may be used for hair. Eyes may be made with beads or buttons. Other features may be either painted or made from paper and pasted on. Holes should be left at sides for fingers of person working puppets. These may be covered with small mitten-like hands.

RAZOR-BLADE CONTAINER

Made from frozen-juice can. Paint with fingernail brush. Make slit in top for old razor blades.

Toy Basket

Paint half-bushel basket and stencil with another color. Use some letters in alphabet for stencil.

Beanbags

Made from old felt hats in the shape of frogs, fish, etc.

Clown Face

Face made from paper plate. Hat made from construction paper and fastened with paper fastener to paper plate. Hole made in center of plate for balloon nose, which can be blown up from wrong side. Features are made from colored paper.

"Dried Stuff" Picture

Press weeds, leaves, wild flowers, etc., between heavy books for about two weeks. Arrange and mount on construction paper and place in discarded picture frames.

Wall Plaques

Made from three paper plates coated with three coats of gloss enamel black; decorate and shellac.

The Flannel Board

When two pieces of flannel or felt come together, you will notice how they cling to each other. It is on this principle that we make use of a flannel board for visual aids. Flannel boards may be purchased, but they are so inexpensive and easy to construct that every teacher should own one.

Cover any piece of rigid material, such as a beaverboard, with flannel or felt. A flannel board 36″ × 36″ can be seen well in the average classroom. You then cut out figures or pictures you wish to use in building up a story on the board. Paste flannel on the back of the pictures (rubber cement is good for pasting) and they will adhere to the flannel board. As you tell a story or relate an experience to your class, place the figures in sequential order on the board. Children may wish to retell the story, holding the figures and placing them as they tell the story.

A flannel board is also helpful as a visual aid when you wish to construct a map and have children remove certain states.

It is indispensable when teaching fractions. Jimmy may not understand 1/8, but if you make a paper chocolate cake cut in 8 parts and fitted together on your flannel board, Jimmy will be able to see that if he removes 1/8 of the cake, 7/8 are left.

A flannel board, filed away with a manila envelope containing cutouts of reading stories, a map, or sections of a pie can be an invaluable help. Keep your explanation simple and give the children many opportunities to demonstrate with your flannel board.

YARN BALL

Cut two cardboard discs six inches in diameter with cutout center measuring four inches across. Wind regular one-ounce sweater wool (about four skeins) lengthwise on a shuttle notched at each end. The shuttle may be made from a ruler or similar piece of wood. Then wind the wool tightly around the discs (together). When completely wound, the center hole will be almost filled. Cut outer edge of wool with a razor blade, slip strong cord between discs to the center, and tie tightly. Tear away the cardboard, and fluff out the wool.

CHAPTER 8

Audio-Visual Aids; Games; Books

Audio-visual aids are commonly used for two purposes: instruction and time consumption. The teacher who uses films or film strips just to keep the children quiet and amused, automatically classifies himself in the baby-sitting category. School time and all teaching devices within that time are to be used for pupil instruction. Any visual aid is as good as the teacher preparation accompanying it. A legitimate question for any teaching film is "Why are you using this?" A child may be diverted by a cartoon for twenty minutes, but unless he was prepared to see it and understand the purpose for

which it was shown and unless it was discussed afterwards, there may be very little learning.

Audio-visual aids usually mean films, film strips, an opaque projector, a record player, and a tape recorder. In using any one or all of these the teacher should endeavor to preview his material before he uses it with the class. It would be embarrassing to be confronted with material not readily explicable or inappropriate for the age level. Anticipate.

Film strips are particularly valuable because the teacher can easily hold a frame for careful examination or reverse it for purposes of review. Films are apt to present a more rapid and temporarily vivid impression, and are used with especial success in the middle and upper grades. An opaque projector will enable a teacher to use a single, beautifully illustrated book for group reading. Everyone then can enjoy the pictures and read the text individually or as a group. And if the teacher who turns the pages has a well-manicured hand with a pretty ring, why, that just lends enchantment to an unusual lesson!

For kindergarten one can use film strips without captions, dealing with the circus, the zoo, the farm (to replace a field trip or supplement a story).

For primary grades, film strips supplementary to the basic readers, as well as those dealing with simple science, nature, and geography, can be used (for group reading and as a supplement for almost any form of textbook material).

In the middle and upper grades a variety of films, film strips, and slides is used to reinforce classroom teaching, stimulate interest in a new unit, and serve as supplementary material for current events and library books or as a summation of work already studied.

By the time a child finishes elementary school he should be visually familiar with the appearance of such famous landmarks as the pyramids of Egypt, the Washington Monument, the New York City skyline, the Arc de Triomphe, the ceiling of the Sistine Chapel, the ruins of the Coliseum, the canals of Venice. He will need this sort of education, for today we live in a very small world, and that

little tow-headed fellow who sits and squirms in the second row of your sixth grade will grow up almost overnight. A few more years and he may well be in the armed forces and seeing for himself the very spots that you first showed him on a classroom screen. Because of you, he may look at them with understanding eyes, familiar friends from out of the past.

Not all the visual aids needed in a classroom must be obtained commercially. Here is a list which includes the minimum equipment each teacher should acquire before he signs a contract:

1. Two hundred pictures encompassing the following areas (these must all be mounted before posting on a bulletin board):

science	pets	health
weather	hobbies	safety
seasons	famous places	holidays
family life	famous people	travel

2. A collection of road maps, topographical maps, a world map.
3. An assortment of worn sheets, pillowcases, and such to be used· for maps. These are used in the lower grades for simple trips to the store or to the firehouse; the middle and upper grades outline them carefully first and do more complicated subjects pertaining to literature or geography. All of these are done in colored wax crayons; when these are ironed, the colors sink into the fabric and become almost like a dye.
4. An assortment of travel brochures, picture post cards, timetables.
5. A number of pictures of the cartoon variety, so that children in the fourth through sixth grades can learn to interpret such forms of art.
6. A fairly large globe for current events, history, geography.
7. A flannel board (also called flannel graph).
8. Puppets. These are hand figures made from small paper or cotton bags and are animated by the thumb and fingers of one hand. A white candy bag and black crayon will make a ghost puppet; any vivid line drawing of a face mounted on a simple bag will serve much the same purpose. Bits of wool, buttons, yard for manes, tails, and whiskers—all can be used advantageously, limited only by the imagination of the teacher. In a primary grade, the teacher can talk seriously to the puppet in his hand in this manner:

> *Teacher:* Good morning, black kitty, it's a rainy day today, isn't it?
>
> *Black k:* Good morning, Miss Moore. Yes, it is raining outside. But today is a good day to play games. I know a fine game for children to play on rainy days.
>
> *Teacher:* Thank you very much, black kitty, but we can't play any games because the room is too noisy. The boys and girls could not listen to the directions.

Black k: Just wait a minute, Miss Moore. Let's think. If each child stopped talking and sat and listened, the room would be very quiet. Sh-h-h-h. All the boys and girls are listening.

Teacher: Thank you, black kitty. We can play a game now.

This is one way in which a puppet can be used; it will also serve to dramatize material in the basic reader, tell the story of the life of a great man, or introduce holidays. A particularly effective puppet for Hallowe'en is made from a rubber ball. The ball itself is painted to resemble a face with long, flowing yarn hair and topped by a peaked black paper hat. A hole in the base of the ball is just large enough for an index finger to be inserted. Wanda, the witch, is a little frightened. This will be her first Hallowe'en. For a long time now she has been learning how to ride her broomstick, and frighten people and haunt houses. This has been hard work; but tonight is the night, and she feels just a little nervous.

Upper-grade children enjoy making more complicated puppets, and will frequently use them to tell stories to the lower grades.

9. Planned field trips. A good teacher will have a list of places to visit *which he has visited first*. No trip should be made without a purpose, prior preparation, and classroom discussion following the trip.
10. Charts.
11. Library books to recommend.
12. Simple science equipment.
13. Collections (of almost any sort) for classroom exhibits.

AUDIO-VISUAL BIBLIOGRAPHY

AUDIO-CARDALOG, Box 1771, Albany 1, N.Y. Subscribers receive cards giving source, grade level, and an evaluation of film. These are planned for filing, giving you a cumulative source of information readily available.

LANDERS FILM REVIEWS, 4930 Coliseum St., Los Angeles 16, Calif. This company publishes a valuable annual issued as a complete volume.

It gives a complete listing of films with sufficient commentary to help the teacher select the best film for her own class.

BROWN, JAMES W., LEWIS, RICHARD B., and HARCLEROAD, FRED F. *A-V Instruction Materials and Methods*. New York, McGraw-Hill, 1959. This is an outstanding example of explicit writing. A teacher who follows and studies the suggestions in this book will be well qualified for classroom work in visual aids.

HINTS FOR THE PRESENTATION OF GAMES

1. Place group in desired formation before any explanation of game is given.
2. Don't talk too long; get to the game itself.
3. In explaining the game, demonstrate. Use a partner, if necessary.
4. Teach intricate games in parts.
5. Encourage now and then; be patient in pointing out mistakes. Call attention to errors rather than to the person making them.
6. Direct attention to the game rather than to yourself as leader.
7. Encourage everyone to play, but do not insist. If a person does not choose to play, assume that he has good reasons for not doing so. If this situation persists, a private conference may be needed.
8. When an activity does not "take hold" for some reason or other (mood, inability, or lack of time to master it), move quickly to another game or activity.
9. When a game fails to interest, examine your own attitude first; be hesitant to blame the group.
10. Stop the game while interest is still strong and players enthusiastic.
11. Be firm but kind in enforcing the rules.
12. Use an outline; don't trust your memory for a day's program.
13. Have extra material ready for use in emergencies. This is foresight.
14. Have all properties ready but never give them out until time for them to be used.
15. Be tolerant, but not so tolerant that "anything goes."
16. Avoid ridicule and "picking on" individuals.

17. Enjoy what you are doing; then others will enjoy it with you.
18. Start with the simple form; then add variations.
19. Observe and try to understand the nature of individual children as released through the informality of games: fear, awkwardness, cheating, bullying, and their opposites—good sportsmanship, fairness, cooperation. Games make teaching easier.

Following are examples of good word-and-action games for various ages:

EVERYBODY DO THIS

Age group: 3 years to 8 years
Formation: Any formation
Action: The leader starts the action and the group has to do that action; while the leader is demonstrating the action he sings a song (words are below). Participants from the group can lead the others when they have caught on to the game. Following are listed six actions which may be used:
1. Pat head, rub stomach.
2. Pyramid, one hand over the other.
3. Grab elbows alternately.
4. Cross and uncross hands on knees.
5. Hop around.
6. Bend and touch toes.
Words: Everybody do this, do this, do this,
Everybody do this, just like me!
Everybody do this, do this, do this,
Everybody do this, just like me![1]

FIVE LITTLE DUCKS

Age group: 6 years to 10 years
Formation: Any formation
Action:
1. Five Little Ducks that I once knew,
(point to self)

[1] Helen J. Fletcher, *Finger Play Poems and Stories.* Darien, Conn., Educational Pub. Co., 1958. For each poem, there are finger-play instructions under the lines to which they apply. These poems may also be used for dramatic play.

Fat ones, skinny ones
   (hands apart, hands together)
There were two,
   (hold up two fingers)
But the one little duck
   (hold up one finger)
With a feather on his back,
   (hand on hip to signify tail)
He led the others with a "Quack, quack, quack."
   (hands on waist and move arms back and forth to show wings)

2. Down to the river they would go,
   (weave hand in and out)
Wiggle-wobble, Wiggle-wobble, to and fro.
   (shift weight back and forth on legs)
But the one little duck,
   (hold up one finger)
With the feather on his back,
   (same as verse one)
He led the others with a "Quack, quack, quack."[2]
   (same as verse one)

SKIP TO MY LOU

Age group: 8 years to 14 years
Formation: A single circle of partners
Action: One couple steps into the circle with an extra player; the three hold hands and skip about the circle. The couple stops and holds joined hands high while the third person, on the word "Skip," steps under the arch thus formed. The couple joins the circle, and the person left in the ring calls in another couple and takes one of the new members for a partner. Together they make the arch and join the circle, leaving alone the other player; he then chooses another couple, and so on to the end of the song.

Words:
1. Flies in the buttermilk, Two by two, flies in the buttermilk, Shoo, fly, shoo, flies in the buttermilk, Two by two, Skip to my Lou, my darlin'.
2. Little red wagon painted blue (etc.).

[2] Words readily adaptable to improvised tune.

3. Can't get a redbird, a bluebird'll do (etc.).
4. Cat's in the sugarbowl, shoo, fly, shoo (etc.).
5. She is gone and I'll go too (etc.).[3]

TENNESSEE WIG WALK

Age group: 9 years to 13 years
Formation: Standing position with a partner
Action:

1. I'm a bow-legged chicken,[4]
   (feet outward)
   I'm a knock-kneed hen,
   (knees together)
   Ain't had no lovin' since I don't know when,
   (shake head—hug yourself—shake head)
   I walk with a wiggle and a giggle and a squawk,
   (bend back; put right heel out, left heel; right heel, left heel)
   Doing the Tennessee Wig Walk
   (put hands on knees and push backward two times; clap hands
   and bring them outward)

CHORUS

   Put your toes together, your knees apart,
   Bend your back, get ready to start,
   Flap your elbows just for luck,
   And you wiggle and you waddle like a baby duck.
   (act with the words)

2. Play a tune on a fiddle on a hardwood floor,
   (stamp foot on floor and pretend to play a fiddle)
   Oh I'm tired and I'm weary and my back is sore.
   (bend over and let your arms go; bend back and hold it with a
   hand)
   I walk with a wiggle (etc.).

CHORUS

[3] The music for this well-known tune can be found in many collections of folk songs for children.
[4] The sheet music version of "The Tennessee Wig Walk" can be acquired at most music stores.

3. Dance with me honey won't you be my guy,
     (with partner dance three steps forward)
   And we'll always be together side by side.
     (put arms around each other and knock hips)
   I walk with a wiggle (etc.).
   CHORUS

PRESENTATION OF BOOKS

How can a teacher know whether his efforts to interest children in books have been successful? He is in a position similar to a preacher's. He may have planned his sermon well and presented it in a most impressive manner. Then he must hope that during the weeks to come, some of his statements will have been comforting or inspirational to his congregation. He cannot ask his parishioners as they

leave the church to evaluate. Neither can a teacher at any grade level anticipate how his well-planned book program will motivate his children to further literary efforts.

We can predict that children whose teacher shares books as a part of his daily program will speak better, use their library cards frequently, find research easy, and even attempt to write stories. Truly the realization that his teacher enjoys a book is the best evidence a child has that reading can be fun.

Reading is a little like creative writing. First, interest must be aroused, according to the child's individual experience and preference. Having captured his interest, the teacher will find that his task of instruction becomes infinitely easier. The individuality of each pupil is inescapable. He can be led, but seldom driven.

For example, children of ages six to eight will tend to be interested in animal stories, stories of children and familiar experiences, nature and simple fairy stories. They prefer their stories to be lively, to have elements of surprise and humor.

At about age nine, the interests of boys and girls usually begin to differ. About this time, boys begin to prefer stories of adventure, mystery, sports, and realistic animal stories. For some boys, interest in science may become strong. Girls, however, seem to prefer stories about home and school life and children of other lands.

These findings are just a few of the generalizations found in studies of children's reading interests. The findings from such studies are helpful in suggesting books for a classroom library or for an individual child. But it is not uncommon to find a second grader asking for an adventure story and a fifth grader interested in a fairy tale.[5]

Remember that children's books are like children's shoes; you cannot be sure that a certain shoe will fit because it is to be worn by a ten-year-old. Neither can we say this book is suitable for all fifth graders. At this age, some girls may prefer to wear striped playshoes, while others may prefer high heels and open-toed styles to affect

[5] Jeanne Chall, "Ask Him to Try on the Book for Fit." In *The Reading Teacher*. Newark, Delaware, International Reading Assoc., 1953.

maturity. How, under these conditions, can a teacher present books so that all his class will enjoy reading?

1. Be sure the children are comfortable before you begin to read or talk about the book. Start with a simple book; hold it up for them to see.
2. Be sure you have enjoyed it yourself. Children like to chuckle with the teacher over a humorous incident.
3. Stop reading the book while interest is high. Then recommend that this book be withdrawn from the library. Permit the children to examine the book before you return it to the library
4. Have other books ready if the first books do not appeal to the class. Present only a few new books at a time. Too many innovations invite confusion in young minds.
5. With each book, mention a few others on a similar topic or by the same author. If a child likes an author, he is apt to read for that reason alone.
6. A brief anecdote about the author is always enjoyable.
7. Involve your students in sharing books. Ask their opinions, listen to their comments, be enthusiastic together.
8. Children will read many books if they are not expected to produce a voluminous book report on each. You will recall the first grader at the zoo who nudged his pal and said, "Don't see too many animals, or you'll have to paint them all for her when we get back."

CHAPTER 9

Parent-Teacher Relationships

Years ago the American public schools were considered a melting pot; today we are witnessing a period when public opinion is causing them to become pressure cookers. Teachers and parents need to know each other better. The parent has a loving and protective interest in the child; the teacher is a professional educator, and as such, should remember that he has—or should have—an aura of pedagogical dignity. A parent-teacher conference is a professional consultation.

If the work concerns the lower grades, the teacher will have samples of drawing or some form of art, samples of manuscript writing, and any other written material. In the upper grades, the

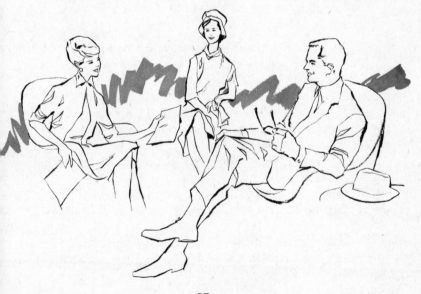

folder for a parent conference should contain several samplings from each of the following areas: arithmetic, spelling, science, creative writing, and evidences of reading achievement.

SOME SUGGESTIONS FOR A SUCCESSFUL INTERVIEW

1. Make parent ready by specific statements.
2. Recognize two points of view.
3. Listen carefully and sympathetically.
4. Do not let it become a pseudo-psychiatric hour.
5. Accept parent plan if possible.
6. Stick to the problem (school).
7. Summarize the interview and try to come up with some specific suggestions for home and school to follow.

Materials needed:
   file cards
   folders
   samples of work in each area, including handwriting
   any memos you may have made during first eight weeks (usual report period)

Fifty percent of the time *you* listen. Many things will come out of your listening period—birth injuries, many illnesses, child's dislike of something in your room. (One mother complained, "You never let him be the Fox in that game you play.")

Quickly make a memo of promises made, information gleaned, etc., before the next parent comes. Consult these *tomorrow*; they will influence your plan book and procedures.

During the next eight-week period make quick notes and follow up suggestions:

"Thank you for the tip. I've given Joe chance to be the fox—you were right, he was resentful." (Note sent to mother after a few days.)

"Note reversal in writing—please see me before letting him write at home." (Note sent to mother on the back of a paper the child handed in.)

SUGGESTIONS FOR THE EVALUATION
OF INTERVIEWS

Some do's

1. Did you plan for a constructive "next step"? Did you accept the suggestions of the parent whenever possible?
2. Did you listen more than you talked?
3. Did you prepare for the interview? Define its purpose? Review pertinent information? Mentally define possible approaches to the parent?
4. Did you present your data, beliefs, and suggestions to the parent when he was ready for it? Did you refrain from giving unasked advice?
5. Did you reach a definite agreement about what each of you will do?

Some don'ts

1. Don't ignore the real concerns of parents.
2. Don't expect too much from one interview.
3. Don't give a monologue.
4. Don't use educational "gobbledegook."

If you are a kindergarten teacher, parents of registered children will appreciate a letter from you about the last week of August. It can read something like this:

Northfield Elementary School
East Lynn, Massachusetts
August 17, 196_

Dear Mr. and Mrs. Jones,

Summer is coming to a close, and school will begin next month. I would like to take this opportunity to welcome your Susan into my kindergarten class at Northfield School.

You are probably wondering just what your child will be doing in kindergarten. Her activities will include: a working period where she will be using blocks, paints, clay, crayons, and tools; a talking and singing period; a listening period which includes listening to stories, music, directions, ideas and suggestions; a looking period where she will find answers to her many questions; a playing period where she will learn to play with others and share her toys; a resting period; and a visiting period when she will visit rooms in the school and places in the community.

There are several things that Susan will need to help her while she is in school:

1. a rug or blanket upon which to lie during rest time;
2. an apron or old shirt to protect her clothing while she paints;
3. a sweater that can be kept at school for use on cool days;
4. a box of paper handkerchiefs or a clean handkerchief each day;
5. clothes that are comfortable and simple for active work and play;
6. clothes which she can fasten and unfasten herself so that she may be independent in this respect;
7. loops sewn on clothing so that she can hang it properly on hooks;
8. her name on clothing and rubbers so that they are less likely to be lost;
9. rubbers large enough so that she can put them on and take them off easily; and
10. a written excuse from home following any absence.

We are happy to have parents visit kindergarten; however, the school suggests that the first visit be not sooner than a month after Susan has entered school. It is much easier for a child to adjust to her new environment if her mother leaves her at the door of the classroom.

If you have any other questions, please feel free to contact me. I'll be looking forward to meeting you at our first parents' conference.

Sincerely yours,

(Miss) Ima Gude Teechr

For the sake of your professional pride, *be sure that you have a correct letter form, the proper punctuation and wording, and no misspelled words*. Now, take your carefully prepared letter to your principal for approval before you do anything more. He must be fully cognizant of all communications sent out officially from the school, or he may find himself in an embarrassing situation and unable to defend the thoughtlessness of his teachers.

The question may arise, "How can I have interviews with the parents of kindergarten children?" All that we have suggested about folders containing samples of writing, arithmetic, and maps could not apply to this age.

After you have discussed any items pertaining to health, adjustment or to other children or emotional problems, you might feel the following topics are of value:

1. Is he well rested?
2. Are you genuinely interested in anything he takes home or any item he reports?
3. Does he feel loved at all times, even when he is punished?
4. Have you established with him an eagerness to see what the next day in his kindergarten will offer?

Not all children are eager to go every day, yet the kindergarten is the place to establish daily attendance. We knew one little boy who awaited eagerly his first day of kindergarten. The next day when his mother called him to get up, he asked—"What, again?"

If you care to discuss items in your kindergarten curriculum, you could explain that you have formed "clubs" with your children. You become a member of the "color club" as soon as you can identify the basic colors in the room.

You may belong to the "address club" when you can give your address.

You may also belong to the "counting club" when you can count to ten.

It might be well, since "show and tell" has become a part of the daily schedule in primary grades, to explain your feeling about it. It would seem to be a national disease whereby children waste 20 to 30 minutes showing *anything* to the class. "Show and tell," of course, must be a form of education or it has no legitimate place in a school day. Here is a variation that has proved its worth in many a classroom:

A "surprise box" fulfills the child's wish to share but can be much more valuable as a way of learning. A large box is placed at a set corner of the room. Any child who wants to bring a toy, book, or souvenir from home may drop it in the box, which has a cover on it.

During discussion period, the teacher or a child may select two or three items to be explained and thoroughly discussed. This permits the teacher to limit the time consumed, and encourage a more concentrated oral discussion centered around a music box from Switzerland or a book of stories from Denmark or a picture Donald drew at home.

Through your brief report on things happening daily in your classroom, parents come to the realization that a kindergarten is not a "waiting room" for the elementary school, but an integral part of the child's education.

FIRST-GRADE CUMULATIVE FOLDERS

"This Is My Life" can be used as the individual cumulative record of a first-grade pupil. It is contained in a legal-size folder, on dated loose sheets. The outside is illustrated and bears the child's name. The first picture may be made on the first day of school, but even the simplest manuscript entries must wait a few weeks. Once the child has learned how to form his letters and label, he may prepare his first entries. One class drew pictures of the teacher on the first day of school; there were thirty pupils, so there were thirty pictures, but each and every one drew the teacher's blue-rimmed spectacles!

As time passes, the folder may contain drawings and captions—dated, of course—such as this:

September   "I can read."
            "The doctor."
            "I can paint."
October   "Leaves fall."
            "See Columbus."
            "See the boats."
            "We made cats." (Hallowe'en)
            "We made faces."
            "We made a witch."
            "We ate apples."
November   "Hello, Mommy." (Parents' Night)
            "Hello, Daddy."
            "This is my seat."

"We went to the store." (Thanksgiving)

"We bought cranberries."

"We made cranberry sauce."

December This month will carry a number of short accounts of a class trip to buy the tree, the decorations of the room, the Christmas play.

January This month may carry a weather diary recording temperature and experiments with ice.

A "story" about My Favorite Christmas Gift will encourage beginning composition.

February This month should give many indications of growth, with writing concerning holidays, weather reports, and Valentine wishes.

March This is a good month for science and class work such as:

"We are making a phone book."

"We can dial numbers."

"I have read seven books."

"Joe has read nine books."

April Here we see an interest in reporting, actual trips, science interests, and personal matters:

"Here I am in my Easter suit."

"Here I am dyeing eggs."

May Here we find plans for May baskets and Mother's Day cards and gifts. This is a good time to plan a "reading party" for mothers.

June Here will be the concluding entries and plans for the summer. This should be self-explanatory, in contrast with early work.

A folder such as this serves a triple purpose:

1. The teacher, in examining past work, is enabled to plot the future. He is able to evaluate the child's learning quite objectively.

2. The child is able to see his own progress and to compete against himself.

3. A parent sees very little work brought home in first grade, and is seldom able to evaluate his child's progress from what he does see. A folder dramatizes developing skills and contributes to parent cooperation and understanding.

PARENT-TEACHER HOMEWORK POLICY

Definition

Homework is an assignment or a portion of an assignment which is to be prepared or completed outside of the classroom.

Purpose of homework

Homework should stimulate the intellectual development of the child and create and broaden desirable interests and habits. It should reinforce the pupil's mastery of skills, expand his store of worthwhile knowledge, encourage creative use of his abilities, and increase his appreciation of the world in which he lives. Homework should be an outgrowth and extension of meaningful classroom activities and help the student to learn how to study.

Role of the teacher

The teacher should provide help in developing good study skills, provide for individual differences and abilities, and make certain that homework assignments are purposeful, clear, and have real meaning for the pupil. Homework should be explained in class to enable pupils to ask questions and to have any initial assistance.

Role of the pupil

The pupil should assume a willing responsibility for completion of homework and should make certain he understands the purpose, requirements, and the method of preparation. He should use study time properly and efficiently, and utilize fully study helps, materials, and resources.

Role of the parent

The parent should try to provide a home atmosphere with facilities conducive to good study. The parent should encourage the child to study and to complete the homework assignments. Parents should give only that kind of assistance and guidance which will enable the child to think for himself in completing his own homework assignments. There should be a mutual understanding of purpose between home and school.

Kindergarten; Grade 1; Grade 2

There should be no specific formal homework in kindergarten, grade 1, and grade 2. However, there may be some enriching experience through related home activities, such as reading of library books, picture interpretation, and storytelling.

Grade 3

Homework may be introduced in grade 3. Assignments should conform to the needs and abilities of pupils.

Grade 4

Assigned homework should be introduced in grade 4. Homework may be assigned three or four times per week. Assignments should require not more than twenty minutes of preparation daily, and should be based on individual needs and abilities of pupils. Development of good home-study habits and learning to study independently should be emphasized at this grade level.

Grade 5

There should be regularly assigned homework in grade 5. Assignments should require not more than thirty minutes of preparation daily and should be based on individual needs and abilities of pupils. Homework assignments should be made no more than three or four times a week.

Grade 6

There should be regularly assigned homework in grade 6. Assignments should require not more than 45 minutes of preparation daily and should be based on individual needs and abilities of pupils. Homework assignments should be made no more than four times a week.

Grades 7 and 8

There should be regularly assigned homework in grades 7 and 8. Homework must, of necessity, be construed to vary from day to day, depending on the nature of the subject matter under discussion and the varying abilities of pupils in different groups. Pupils should be cautioned to be alert for long-range assignments which require careful planning on their part. The following schedule is recommended with the thought that both parents and teachers will recognize the need for attention to individual differences and abilities:

Grade 7, 1 hour to 1 and 1/4 hours daily.
Grade 8, 1 and 1/4 hours to 1 and 3/4 hours daily.

DON'T BLAME THE CHILDREN

We have suggested in describing the role of the parent that he offer encouragement and a minimum of assistance to the child. This can be done only in a home where the atmosphere is conducive to study and where there is an adult present who is ready to guide the child. Much of the responsibility for the actions of children rests on the shoulders of adults.

We read in the paper and hear on the air,
Of killing and stealing and crime everywhere.
We sigh and we say as we notice the trend,
"This young generation. Where will it end?"

But can we be sure that it's their fault alone,
That maybe a part of it isn't our own?
Are we less guilty who place in their way,
Too many things that lead them astray?
Too much money to spend, too much idle time,
Too many movies of passion and crime;
Too many books not fit to be read;
Too much evil in what they hear said;
Too many children encouraged to roam,
By too many parents who won't stay at home.

Kids don't make the movies; they don't write the books,
That paint pictures of gangsters and crooks;
They don't make the liquor; they don't run the bars.
They don't make the laws and they don't buy the cars.
They don't peddle drugs that addle the brain;
That's all done by older folks greedy for gain.
Delinquent teenagers! Oh, how we condemn
The sins of the nation and blame it on them.
For in so many cases it's sad but it's true,
The title "delinquent" may fit older folks, too.[1]

[1] From "Don't Blame the Children." By permission of Garfield Public Schools, Garfield, New Jersey.

CHAPTER 10

How to Enjoy a Day at a Time

An elementary-school substitute may be called upon to teach any grade—kindergarten through eighth. This prospect alone would appall an experienced teacher cognizant of the range of attention span, subject matter, stability, discipline, and daily schedules involved. The substitute is a teacher who arrives for a day or two without the psychological assistance of knowing each pupil's name and administering ultimate justice via the report card. He will need the ingenuity of a European diplomat and the skill of a prestidigitator, plus the enthusiasm of a circus barker. He may even enjoy himself; certainly the children should enjoy him.

In view of the fact that the teacher is the focal point of the classroom, he should be attractive. A well-tailored dress or suit in a becoming color, a neat coiffure, an air of assurance plus a friendly

smile—that's all anyone could want, except for the kit. That kit will be his bag of tricks, his stock in trade, his repertoire. No amount of charm will ever neutralize the fumbling, uncertain approach of an unprepared teacher; hence the kit.

THE INDISPENSABLE KIT

This is a brown cardboard carton, from the local grocery store, with openings cut at each end to serve as handles for easier carrying. The substitute should prepare three of these and label them clearly:

Kgn.1–2 (primary)

3–5 (middle)

6–8 (upper)

These will contain the essentials. If the temporary teacher takes time to look for things, he will lose the interest of the class, so he brings what he plans to use. If he finds additional resources in the classroom, so much the better, but he has come prepared to teach under any circumstances.

Contents basic to each of the three cartons are:

1. thermos and box of crackers or chocolate bar, paper napkins (You may not be able to get out for lunch.)
2. facial tissues (for you and pupils) and ready-made adhesive bandages
3. tube of paste, chalk, cellophane tape, several cheap sharpened pencils, ball point pens
4. paper clips, rubber bands, red pencil, black poster-marking pencil
5. two yarn balls (See section on "Trash or Treasure," p. 61, for directions.)
6. blunt scissors
7. flannel board (made in two sections and hinged for carrying) and manila envelope with figures for mounting (see p. 72)

FOR KINDERGARTEN THROUGH SECOND GRADE

1. story books
2. poetry books (It should, of course, be unnecessary to remind

the teacher that he must have read these books himself and be thoroughly familiar with the contents. Selections for use should be clearly marked.)

3. records—listening and rhythm
4. indoor and outdoor games on cards (A rainy day will double your need for indoor games.)
5. a hand puppet (See bibliography and "Trash or Treasure" section)
6. a sheet of art suggestions for seasons and holidays
7. candy box with small bottles of perfume, camphor, weak ammonia, vinegar, vanilla (for describing smell)
8. candy box with pieces of velvet, fur, satin, sandpaper, aluminum foil, tweed, and gauze (for describing touch)
9. magnifying glass; magnet with iron filings
10. large calendar (for number work)
11. small slips of paper for pupil names, and paper of pins
12. time schedule of each grade on file card
13. a folder of appropriate pictures. Pictures come from everywhere—store displays, calendars, magazines. They should be trimmed, mounted on fresh colored paper, and filed under these categories:

   a. seasons
   b. holidays
   c. toys
   d. pets and zoo animals
   e. famous people
   f. scientific phenomena
   g. unusual events
   h. humorous scenes
   i. magazine covers under no particular category, to be used for creative storytelling.

In the primary grades, pictures are used to illustrate stories told by the teacher. They may also be given to individual pupils with the instructions, "Study the picture, and tell the class a story about it." This serves to stimulate the imagination and strengthen the vocabulary.

FOR GRADES THREE THROUGH FIVE

1. map (world)
2. copies of current children's magazines
3. flash cards for arithmetic drills
4. flash cards for vocabulary drill taken from Dolch or Gates word lists, augmented with key words from basic texts used in classroom.
5. folder of pictures to be used for:
   a. who's who bulletin board
   b. creative storytelling and writing
6. a simple folk dance record
7. games on file cards (indoor and outdoor)
8. a weekly TV and radio guide for class discussion
9. a good collection of folk tales to be read (or told, preferably) by the teacher
10. a sheet of seasonal science questions
11. science "equipment" to be augmented by teacher's basic knowledge:
    a. magnifying glass
    b. small container of mercury
    c. interesting minerals and rocks
    d. coins
    e. litmus paper, vinegar, laundry bleach, etc.
12. a sheet of suggestions for art work
13. a time schedule of each grade on file cards
14. a poetry anthology (passages marked)
15. small pocket dictionary

FOR GRADES SIX THROUGH EIGHT

1. large map (world)
2. TV guide for discussion and writing
3. mimeographed sheets for arithmetic drill (answers for quick check)
4. mimeographed sheets for quick reading diagnosis (answers for quick check)

5. record for music appreciation—*1812 Overture, Peer Gynt Suite, Danse Macabre, The Lonesome Train*
6. science material which may serve as catalyst for an entire lesson: e.g., piece of lava, pages of a book in galley proof or uncut sheets from bindery, coin collections, mementos from various wars, animal skull and replica of human skull. Only one or two of these may be carried at a time, but each needs to serve as the nucleus of a lesson, as:

Piece of Lava

geological formation and names (magma and lava)
hypothesis of earth's center
constituents of lava—testing for iron with magnet
geographical location of volcanos
dramatic history of Pompeii
modern pineapple plantations and volcanic soil

This same technique may be applied to any one of the above science topics. This is the grade level of the bright, scientific-minded boy who may be better informed than his teacher, who may capture his interest and respect, hence his classroom co-operation, by a thought-provoking science presentation.

7. mimeographed sheets to correlate current events with geo-graphical locations. This age group can utilize more individual study and paper work than younger groups.

When a substitute first enters a school he should locate or inquire about:

a. fire regulations and exits
b. lavatory facilities and school regulations regarding their use
c. use of playground and gymnasium
d. times of opening, recess, and dismissal
e. lunch regulations and facilities
f. schedules of special teachers (art, music, physical education) for that day
g. class register
h. record player
i. ventilation

No substitute will ever change the pattern of any class in a day. He is a teacher "taking over" for the time being, and goes prepared to have the children respect and enjoy him. This should never be considered "baby-sitting" or a time for "busy" work; the substitute has an opportunity for real teaching in his own way, and genuine learning can take place.

The first hour or so is always used to gain rapport, learn names, and establish discipline. Group work, independent activities, and peer tutoring will necessarily come later. Ingenuity and a sense of the integration of all knowledge are essential for any teacher, but for a substitute both of these *plus* anticipation are required. He who does not anticipate may be surprised!

A substitute may question the advisability of spending money to equip kits, but one day spent in a classroom without materials would convince him of the wisdom of the expenditure.

And just as a car carries a spare tire in case of trouble, a substitute may like to have a few reminders, just in case:

1. In primary grades, to introduce himself, he can use this jingle:

> _____is my name.
> Your name I hope to know;
> I was happy when I came,
> I'll be sad when I must go.

2. Many disciplinary problems would not arise if the teachers had foreseen situations and prepared the children to meet them. Children do not care to be surprised. They need to be prepared for the next step.
3. Always go over seatwork with children before they work alone.
4. Don't point with your fingers. Use a marker for both board and individual book work in order to:
    emphasize left to right motion
    keep the eyes from wandering
    designate phrase groupings rather than single words.
5. Give each child affection; remember he is only 72 months old in first grade.
6. (primary grades) Try saying the alphabet in unison; children enjoy it as much as they do counting to a hundred.
7. Reading is serious business. It cannot be taught in a tower of Babel.

8. Dipping a paint brush in water and writing on the board is a good way to practice manuscript writing. A pupil may write a word and the game may be to read what has been written before the water evaporates and the word disappears.

9. If the teacher doesn't like what he is doing, how can the children?

CHAPTER 11

The Twelve Most Important Questions

A recent poll of first-year teachers revealed numerous anxieties, and several questions appeared so frequently in answer to the questionnaire that it may be reasonable to assume that they are of concern to many teachers:

1. *What can I do with the slow reader?*
First ascertain just how slow the child is, by *testing*. Rule-of-thumb comparison with other children in the class is not advisable. Let us suppose that Johnny is in fifth grade and tests 2.4. (In other words, his test results place him at second year, fourth month.)

The teacher's first job is to start Johnny in books suitable for his reading level and acceptable to the interests of his age. If he is interested in cowboys, he will not enjoy reading about the troubles of an Easter rabbit. The books given to him should be new material, not part of the classroom reading series. He should keep a personal chart of his reading in which he competes against his own achievement, and have an allotted time *daily* in which he reports to the teacher and reads for her ear alone.

His teacher may even keep his "log," for which he dictates experiences of the day to him. This record is done in manuscript writing because of its similarity to regular type. Cursive writing is almost always difficult for the slow reader. Reading and re-reading this log is a source of great enjoyment to a youngster and will greatly enrich his sight vocabulary.

The teacher will continuously strive to remind such a pupil of

his need to read just a little more in reaching toward his potential. He will take the trouble to include him somehow in all class work. Upon occasion, the child may read his science or social-studies lesson to one of the more advanced pupils. All reading, all interest, all improvement will add up to success, and *confidence*, you remember, is the memory of past successes.

2. *How important is reading, anyway?*

The author firmly believes that no normal child should be permitted to leave the primary grades without the ability to read. Like Tennyson's "Brook," other interests may come and interests go, but reading, in some form, must go on daily.

To emphasize this again in the echo of familiar words: "Neither Christmas, nor Hallowe'en, nor Valentine's Day, should stop the daily reading schedule in the primary class."

One never learns to play the piano well without daily practice. A child cannot learn to read by haphazard instruction. Every day must carry with it new experiences and new vocabulary.

3. *How should I arrange the seating in my classroom?*

Children seem to work better when they sit near their friends. Let them sit where they choose at first, but if there is any undue talking or misbehavior, quietly but firmly assign that child to another seat.

4. *How can I learn to remember all my children's names?*

In the upper grades, have the youngsters make name tags for their seats. A rectangle of light cardboard may be folded in half lengthwise and the name of the child printed on each side. When school begins each day, this name tag should be placed on a corner of the desk until the teacher feels that he knows the name, and gives permission for it to be removed. This should be kept in the desk throughout the year and displayed whenever the special teachers come to visit the class or a substitute is necessary.

In the lower grades the names are written on paper fish or sail-

boats and pinned on clothing with safety pins. For the first two months these are to be worn to and from school by all small bus riders for the convenience of the bus driver as well as the teacher.

5. How do I arrive at marks?

Marking is largely a matter of personal opinion on the part of the teacher. Grades are colored by the teacher's aims and impressions of a child's progress, his interest, his nuisance value, his parents and their interest in the child, his ability, his effort, his testing results, his performance with his peers.

6. How do I build vocabulary?

Vocabulary is mainly built through the eyes and the ears. A child may become accustomed to hearing a new word and understanding its meaning; but if he has never seen that word, it may seem completely strange to him until it is pronounced. A child who has learned a new word only through his reading may mispronounce it because he has only seen it, never heard it in context. If a teacher uses a new word verbally he must always write it on the board as well. If the usage tends to be idiomatic, such as adjacent *to*, or *in* agreement *with*, a phrase should be employed. Vocabulary tends to stem from imitation; therefore, the word should be correctly phrased and pronounced the very first time it is used.

Vocabulary emanates from an enriched curriculum. The teacher must go beyond the text into the realm of advertising, newspapers, and television. Vocabulary is vital to understanding; it is part of listening, part of seeing; it should be natural, frequently repeated, and *part of every day*.

7. *How do I handle choral speaking?*

First you select the poem. In the primary grades, it should have rhythm and rhyme and have a certain amount of repetition. There should be parts for different groups of high or low voices and repetitive portions for the entire class. Onomatopoeia (words that imitate sounds) is especially desirable for primary grades and can be used with motion.

Choral speaking teaches listening: first to the original of the poem, then to the teacher's instructions as the group learns individual portions, and finally to themselves as recorded on tape. Choral speaking teaches cooperation: each child blends his voice with the group's; each watches the director for signals, starts and stops promptly. Choral speaking is particularly good for the shy child, for clear phonetic enunciation, and for demonstration at school assemblies and P.T.A. gatherings.

8. *How can I make my teaching more colorful?*

First of all, enjoy it yourself; laugh frequently, if you can share a joke together. Wear fresh, pretty clothes and a becoming hair-do if you are a woman. If you are a man, neatly pressed clothes, a fresh shirt daily, and a frequent change of tie are essential. After all, if the children are bored, remember it is *you* that they watch all day. Your appearance and attitude take precedence over the subject matter.

Find something new and interesting to share each day. The world is a fascinating place; share it with your pupils. If you find an interest in the air age and you have spent the previous evening reading about rockets, you can do something like this: rockets are built around

Newton's third law—i.e., for every action there is an equal reaction.
A rocket goes forward because an equal amount of energy is being
released in the opposite direction. A shotgun kicks when it is fired.
It reacts in the direction which is opposite to velocity of the fired
bullet. This is how a rocket goes up—or wherever it goes. A class
from fourth grade up will enjoy simple scientific experiments, particularly when they are readily applicable to the daily news.

In the primary grades, try discussing something alive and wiggly.
A little garter snake or turtle is fascinating and wonderfully made:
what is his tongue for? how does he move? what is he like inside?
how does he see? do garter snakes or turtles really lay eggs?

Take a good book—or two—and show the pictures; read a little,
then put it on the library table in the back of the room. If your
children enjoy it enough, perhaps one of them may enjoy reading
it to some members of a lower grade.

Bring some seashells to school and explain them in an interesting fashion, one by one. Use pictures or drawings as well as the board, to help your explanation. Let the children handle them.

Bring examples of semiprecious and simulated stones to school and show how a royal crown looks when it is set with rubies, pearls, emeralds, and sapphires. A surprising number of children go completely through grammar school without knowing the colors of turquoise, garnet, topaz, or amethyst. Stones such as this make a fascinating discussion and enrich the vocabulary. Write the words on the board (remember?).

Even the common milkweed pods give a lesson in seed dispersal. A soft breeze will carry the delicate particles and scatter them as nature intended. Seeds are all around us, in acorns, apple cores, and pine cones, and each one can become part of a lesson.

Dramatize some of your favorite stories on a rainy afternoon. Keep a storage box of quick costume helps, such as feathers, a rubber dagger, a few hats, a long skirt or two, a colorful sash or belt, and you have the makings of an imaginative hour.

Let the children examine things for themselves. Feeling is part of learning. If you doubt this at all, observe the actions of any woman shopper. She looks, she feels, then she decides whether or not to make the purchase. All learning comes through the senses; the more colorful, the more it will appeal to the senses and finally come to rest as part of an intellectual experience in the life of a child.

9. *How can I get along with parents?*

It is essential for you to remember that no matter how fond you may be of little Jimmy, you are not his parent. He may seem misunderstood, neglected, or ignorant, but all you can legally do is instruct him during school hours or shortly thereafter, and advise and consult with his parents. He comes from his family and returns to it. Your role is of importance, assuredly, but you can only supplement the family influence, not replace it. Jimmy may move to another town, to another school, to another teacher, but he will take his family with him. It is rather humbling for a teacher to realize the limitations of his importance in the life of a growing child, and how his influence must be adapted and altered to fit the mold of that child's life. Years and years later a grown man may remember the loving care of a teacher, but in images that would not be recognizable to the original. A good teacher is one who accepts the fact that he may be forgotten.

A child's parents and home are a unit. When you meet with his parents, try to remember that you, your educational background, your schoolroom, and your way of thinking may be quite baffling to them. Talk with both parents, if possible; two heads may understand you better than one. If you are invited to the home for coffee or tea, go. It will help you to help your pupil, because you will comprehend more of the basic influences in his life.

10. *How can I teach my children to spell?*

Spelling is taught in the primary grades and continues throughout the elementary school. From current comments, perhaps it should become a part of the secondary school curriculum as well. At the very beginning, a child is made word-conscious. The teacher draws his attention to the appearance of the word.

Words, like people, come in different shapes and sizes. This is

part of the basic reading training for word recognition, but here the resemblance ends. Reading is a broader and quicker process than spelling.

Spelling is exact. Just as a male adult is a man, a man may be Mr. Smith. But then again, he may not; the difference is important. Mr. Smith and Mr. Jones may even be the same height and weight and look alike. But Mr. Jones has gray hair and wears glasses. There is a difference; he is certainly not Mr. Smith. So it is with words; spelling is concerned with these small but vital differences. A single letter can change everything and a child must be able to see this.

There are four universal rules for learning to spell:

1. hearing it correctly
2. seeing it written correctly
3. pronouncing it correctly
4. writing it correctly

These serve the auditory, visual, oral, and kinesthetic senses. The first of these is overworked and the last sadly neglected. Never underestimate the kinesthetic sense as a device of teaching; it is most effective. So effective, in fact, that if you permit a child to write a mispelled word ten times, and he writes it ten times in a new misspelling which is an attempt to correct the original error, you have undoubtedly made your contribution to the shame of the written word in American public schools.

Once the pupil has begun the habit pattern of correctly spelling a word, reinforce that habit continuously. Give snap quizzes, use it in board exercises, point it out in the reading. Always give the pupils a spelling test with some scrap paper in addition; visual memory should help give them the correct choice of a word. In showing the differences between the correct and incorrect spelling of a word, always cross out the incorrect spelling; strengthen the correct visual memory.

The child who does not pronounce the ending of a word probably will not spell it with the ending. He must hear himself say it first, and hear the ending—not once, but many times. Practice in distinct pronunciation helps spelling.

A poor reader is axiomatically a poor speller, for spelling is more complex than reading, and English is not a language which offers absolutes in word construction, meaning, or pronunciation. If the child can't read, how can you expect him to spell? Routine spelling is probably best taught in word families—i.e., prefix and suffix. If the pupil can learn to spell the basic word, he should be able to spell variations of that word with little difficulty.

certain	ready	willing
certainly	readiness	unwilling
uncertain	unready	unwillingness
uncertainty	readily	unwillingly
		and so on.

Spelling tests given in correct phrasing help; dividing a word into syllables helps; rhyming helps; in the end, the eyes will make the decision.

The following list contains, in syllables, the most commonly misspelled words. Each grammar-school child should be well drilled in the correct spelling of such words before he enters secondary education. The few unfamiliar words in the list will serve as essential vocabulary enrichment:

ab sence	al ready	ar riv al	can di date
ac cept	al tar	ar ti cle	can vass (*verb*)
ac ci den tal ly	al ter (*change*)	ath let ics	cap i tal (*city*)
ac com mo date	al to geth er	at tacked	capi tol (*building*)
ac cus tom	al ways	au thor	cap tain
ache	am a teur	awk ward	car ry ing
a chieved	a mong	be fore	ceil ing
ac quaint ed	a mount	be gin ning	cem e ter y
ac quired	an gle	be lieve	cer tain
a cross	an swer	ben e fit ed	change a ble
ad dress	anxious	breath	chauf feur
ad vice (*noun*)	a pol o gy	breathe (*verb*)	choice
ad vise (*verb*)	ap pa ra tus	Brit ain	choose
aer i al	ap pear ance	bu reau	cho sen
af fect (*influence*)	ap pe tite	bur ied	clothes
ag gra vate	ap pre ci ate	busi ness	coarse (*not fine*)
aisle	arc tic	caf e te ri a	co coa
all right	ar gu ment	cal en dar	colo nel

col umn
com ing
com mit tee
com par a tive
con science
cool ly
coun try
cour te ous
crit i cism
crowd
cur tain
de ceive
def i nite ly
de scent
de scrip tion
de sert
de sir a ble
de spair
des sert (*food*)
de vel op
dif fer ent
din ing
dis ap pear
dis ap point
dis as trous
dis ci pline
dis eases
di vine
does n't
ef fect
eighth
el i gi ble
em bar rass
em pha size
en vi ron ment
e quipped
es pe cial ly
ex ag ger at ed
ex cel lent
ex cept
ex pense

ex pe ri ence
ex treme ly
fa mil iar
Feb ru ar y
fi nal ly
fore head
for eign
for ty
fourth
fresh man
friend
fun da men tal
gen er al ly
ghost
gram mar
griev ance
guar an tee
guard
hand some
height
he roes
hop ing
hu mor ous
hun gry
i mag i na tion
im me di ate ly
in ci den tal ly
in de pend ent
in gen ious
in oc u la tion
in ter fere
its (*possessive*)
it's (*it is*)
jeal ou sy
kin der gar ten
knew
knowl edge
lab o ra to ry
laid
li a ble
li brar y

light ning
lit er a ture
loose
losing
mag a zine
main tain
main te nance
mar riage
math e mat ics
meant
mere ly
min ute
mis chie vous
mis spell
mort gage
mur mur
mys te ri ous
nat u ral ly
nec es sar y
nick el
niece
ninety
no tice a ble
oc ca sion
oc curred
o mit ted
one self
op por tu ni ty
o rig i nal
paid
pam phlet
par al lel
par lia ment
part ner
pas time
pa tience
pe cul iar
per form ance
per haps
per se ver ance
per son al ly

per suade
planned
pleas ant
pos sess
pos si ble
prai rie
pre ced ing
prej u diced
prin ci pal (*chief*)
prin ci ple (*rule*)
priv i lege
prob a bly
pro ceed ed
pro fes sor
pro nun ci a tion
psy chol o gy
pump kin
pur su ing
quan ti ty
qui et
re al ize
re al ly
re ceive
rec og nize
rec om mend
re ferred
rel e vant
re li gious
rep e ti tion
res tau rant
rhythm
sal a ry
sand wich
scarce ly
sched ule
sec re tar y
seize
sen si ble
sep a rate
ser geant
se vere ly

shin ing	suc ceed	to day	villain
sieve	suc cess	too	vol ume
sim i lar	suf fi cient	to ward	weath er
ski ing	sure ly	trag e dy	Wednes day
soph o more	sur prise	tries	weight
speaks	sur round	tru ly	weird
speech	tar iff	Tues day	wheth er
sta tion er y	than	typ i cal	who's (*who is*)
(*paper*)	their	un nec es sar y	whose (*possessive*)
stat ue	there	un til	wom en
stat ure	there fore	u su al ly	writ ing
stat ute	they're	u ten sil	writ ten
stom ach	thor ough ly	val u a ble	you're
strength	those	veg e ta ble	yours (possessive)

11. *What should I do about homework?*

Homework is of value only when it is carefully assigned to rein-force learning or to give added practice to skills learned in class. If given as busy work and filed in the wastebasket, it loses its value. Children soon detect and learn to resent busy work.

12. *What about discipline? My class seems so restless.*

The key to this lies in the teacher's ability to anticipate trouble. Primary children have a very short attention span. Every first-grade teacher would benefit by having a cuckoo clock to mark the quarter hours, reminding him to change the program from quiet work to active work or vice versa. This period gradually expands to about thirty-five or forty minutes in the sixth grade. If cramped muscles are given no relief, if the work is unvaried, children will force the issue and find relief for their cramped muscles by varying the work with mischief.

Children of grammar-school age need the security of a daily schedule. This will take careful planning on the part of the teacher, for while he is handling a reading group, the others must be work-ing on independent assignments. These assignments must be practi-cal, and not haphazard busy work, or the youngsters will busy them-selves according to their own devices.

There are times when the schedule simply will not work, and nothing goes well. The teacher must then be able to call upon his ingenuity and teach some other way.

In Paris, the Arc de Triomphe stands in the Place d'Etoile with streets radiating from it in all directions. Let us suppose that learning, be it reading or arithmetic, is analogous to the Arc de Triomphe. If we approach by one street and find it blocked, we may arrive at our destination by another way. If we know where we want to go, a path is always open.

Discipline is anticipation, in large part, avoiding trouble before it happens. But when order is necessary and right, order should be had. Quietly but firmly spot the trouble-maker and warn him with a look and a shake of the head. If nothing happens, and all reasonable precautions have failed, remove him from the group. Here are a few "don'ts":

1. Don't send him to the principal; that is a last resort. Handle your problems yourself with a quiet talk later.
2. Don't threaten unless you intend to carry out that threat. And carry it out, if you said you would.
3. Don't fail to remember that your lack of sleep, your frayed nerves, and your worries will affect the class.
4. Don't forget that children have problems too. If a well-behaved child becomes a little monster, take it easy. He may have trouble at home.

AND FOR ALL TEACHERS—

Do's

1. Do remember you are the teacher.
2. Do remember "good fences make good neighbors"—keep space between you and your class.
3. Do remember to have children bring in books, samples, and specimens.
4. "Your voice is your fortune"—keep it by keeping it moderate.
5. Do remember that pupils in the upper grades need activity and changes of pace, too.
6. Do invest in such inexpensive items as wire desk baskets for filing. All papers to be marked can be placed in one basket, and papers the teacher is returning in another; this avoids confusion and teaches system.
7. Bulletin boards should be the joint responsibility of teacher and pupils. See that these displays are an example of good taste. A few sheets of colored paper used for mounting make even arithmetic papers artistic.
8. Do you have a beauty spot in your room? In a primary grade, it may be a low table with a small rocking chair so that the occupant can watch the ant colony on the table. (This is a fascinating and instructive science display that can be purchased or made easily.)
9. Give directions once and then *stop*. A fifth grader remarked to a class visitor—"We only listen on the third round—she always gives directions three times."
10. Be quick to praise, slow to punish, *but*—when you have to mete out punishment, do it.
11. Do show enthusiasm. It will help you to "sell" some dull but essential materials even to that overgrown, unenthusiastic sixth grader.
12. Do put out only a few books on the library table for older children. Next week change books.

13. Do put out a few toys, games, and pieces of equipment if you are a kindergarten teacher. Change each week, putting out new materials, tucking away used materials.
14. Do explain to children what you want them to do.
15. Do teach fifth- and sixth-grade children to make a few notes when you are having a lesson, to prepare them for note-taking later. They may also make brief notations on cards when they are doing "research."
16. Do give work of a challenging nature for homework.
17. Do spend ample time preparing before introducing a subject to your class.
18. Do take time to laugh *with* your children, never *at* them.
19. Do remember that education takes place everywhere, not just in school. You are learning, too.
20. Do remember that there is no substitute for drill in the essentials. Well-taught arithmetic facts are never the result of incidental learning.

DONT'S

1. Don't think quietude always indicates learning in your class.
2. Don't spend all the time talking—give children an opportunity to ask questions.
3. Don't present your lesson until it is thoroughly prepared.
4. Don't sacrifice safety in order to use some new "teaching aid."
5. Don't throw away any odds and ends of materials—put them in a box and use for art projects.

CHAPTER 12

And in Conclusion —

"I cannot but remember such things were,
That were most precious to me."
—SHAKESPEARE

Our dining-room table had a red cover with fringe around the edge. It was put on after the dishes had been removed and Father had settled down to read the evening paper while the youngsters did their homework. Or, if it were Friday evening, they played games: checkers, parcheesi, dominoes. Dominoes were fun, and they taught a form of basic arithmetic quite painlessly—practically the same thing that modern education calls "number grouping concepts for the primary grades." In those days, however, it was just called dominoes; and because it was a game, we learned how to be good losers and pleasant winners as well.

A game of dominoes is not easy to purchase today. Only recently two shopkeepers replied, "Pardon? Dom-in-oes? No, I'm afraid we've never carried them." A pity.

The dining-room table was the focal point of our home. It meant more than the food put upon it, for that went only into our stomachs. It was there that we received food for our minds; and that contributed to our maturity. Around that table sat all the people we knew best and trusted most—our parents and relatives, the familiar faces of security. And there is nothing more important than security in the life of a child.

First of all there was the security of knowing that six o'clock brought all the family together; one was expected to be there. The food was home-cooked and brought to a table set for the evening

meal. Father took his seat at the head, Mother at the foot. Each knew his place, young and old alike. Each shared food and ideas; each learned from the other. No one was too young to speak; no one was too old to contribute an opinion. There was a sense of belonging in that family unit. To draw a present-day analogy, consider the set-up of a gang. You have much the same picture without the stability of mature, loving parents. Otherwise the pattern is almost identical, for the need to belong to a group is basic. Only the results will be dissimilar.

What has happened to that dining-room table? It has been replaced by sets of individual television trays, the kitchen table, or the breakfast nook. Food is the common denominator. But as the Bible says, "Man shall not live by bread alone," and so it is with the dining-room table. It is only as worthwhile as the people who sit around it and the love that surrounds it. Food? Food for the body is less important than food for the spirit, and many times the spirit needs to be fed first.

I once remember having a bitter quarrel with my girl friend, each trying to outdo the other. Finally she said a terrible thing for which there was no answer, and as I walked home at supper time, I thought very hard. Suppose it were true, then what? I would never be walking home to my nice supper again. This might be the last time; the last time.

The smell of chicken and dumplings and onions and peas and pie and all the things I liked best came from the kitchen. "You're just in time to set the table," said Mother. She handed me the knives and forks. When the meal was served, I picked up my napkin reluctantly. What would I be eating tomorrow night? Certainly not chicken and dumplings.

"Milk, honey?" said Father. I nodded, but did not touch the glass when it was filled. I was too full of pain to eat. Mother put out her hand and felt my forehead. "You don't seem to have a temperature. What's the trouble?" At this the tears began.

"What do you care if I eat or not! You don't even know who I am! And you never told me. That's worst of all."

Father looked at Mother and they both looked at me. My grandmother was utterly bewildered by the furor. She kept repeating, "What does she mean? I don't know what she means." This only aggravated the whole miserable situation for me.

"Shut up!" I shouted. At this my father spoke sharply.

"Come now, that is no way to speak to your grandmother. She's only trying to understand, the way your mother and I are. Now what's the trouble? Out with it!"

I struggled with my tears and blurted it all in one breath. "You got me out of an ash can. Mary Lou told me so. That's why I have red hair and freckles and you both have brown hair. That's why there's only one of me. An ash can! Why didn't you tell me before this?"

I don't really remember how it all ended, but like everything else, it was discussed at the family dinner table and cleared up to everyone's satisfaction. When I ate my dinner that night it was with appetite, feeling secure in the knowledge that I was indeed my parents' child, and a beloved one.

All tables are not alike, even dining-room tables. I remember well a dinner eaten in the well-to-do home of one of my pupils some time ago. The table gleamed with silver and crystal; there were flowers and candles. Soft music came from another room. The food was delicious; the company delightful. We four adults at the table felt relaxed and congenial and almost forgot the children who were eating in the butler's pantry. In a few minutes the noise from behind that closed door increased to such an extent that the mother questioned the maid. "They're quarreling a bit, and Jack's throwing muffins at his brother, madam."

"Well, tell them to be quiet, or I'll send his teacher out there and she'll settle him in a hurry."

This was not the job of the teacher. A reprimand from me would have been less than nothing, for training at mealtimes begins around the dining-room table and is evidenced there, over a period of years.

The dining-room table of my memory was only a symbol. It could well have been replaced by any other object basically agreeable and serviceable to all. It should have been large enough for all concerned to meet at regular intervals, and versatile enough to function in several ways. What else could it be, really?

It was here, too, that God played a part. I still remember my father looking about him in that brief moment of appraisal. The steaming meat and vegetables had been brought in, the plate of bread, the pitcher of milk—all was in readiness. Then he bowed his head. "All things come from thee, O Lord, and we are truly thankful." After that we ate and talked. Of the two, the latter was the more important, for here was the beginning of learning and the discipline of love.

Often interesting people came to visit us and lingered over the coffee to discuss books and poetry, to reminisce about Europe, to tell anecdotes about the great or near great, or just to exchange ideas. If I kept very quiet, no one seemed aware that I was listening. Coffee, congenial minds, the enchantment of words, all wove themselves into the tapestry of my imagination. It was on one of those good evenings that I first heard "Abou Ben Adhem." The old friend who repeated the words lingered over them as though he relished the beauty of each phrase. We all listened; it was a shared happiness.

... And saw within the moonlight in his room,
Making it rich and like a lily in bloom,
An angel writing in a book of gold;
Exceeding peace had made Ben Adhem bold. . . .

"Exceeding peace"—in a world of tranquilizers and psychiatrists—could loosen tense hands, smooth out the tight lines in faces and slow the pace of hurrying feet.

"Exceeding peace"—perhaps that is the legacy we can give to our children of the atomic age. We can try, at any rate, if we can find the time to seat ourselves as a family—in love and fellowship—around a dining-room table.

You have something to say. Something of your very own. Try to say it. Don't be ashamed of any real thought or feeling you have. Don't undervalue it. Don't let the fear of what others may think of it prevent you from saying it. Perhaps not aloud, but to yourself. You have something to say, something no one else in the world has ever said in just your way of saying it—but the thing itself is not half so important to you as what the *saying* will be to you.[1]

[1] Hughes Mearns, *Creative Power*. New York, Doubleday, 1929. Reprinted by permission of the author.

BIBLIOGRAPHY FOR TEACHERS

BRADLEY, DUANE, and LORD, EUGENE. *Our World of Science*. New York, Lippincott, 1959. Eight chapters of this concise book deal with eight areas of science, while the ninth and last chapter gives the reader a peep into the future world of science.

BROWN, JAMES W., LEWIS, RICHARD B., and HARCLEROAD, FRED T. *A-V Instruction Materials and Methods*. New York, McGraw-Hill, 1959. This volume offers three distinct educational experiences. Part I gives a rich background for the teacher. Part II shows him how to select and use materials; and Part III shows how to create one's own materials. This is a complete and modern all-inclusive course in visual aids.

CROSBY, MURIEL, and HURLEY, BEATRICE DAVIS. *Adventuring with Books*. Champaign, Illinois, National Council of Teachers of English, 1960. This excellent annotated bibliography of children's books would assist any teacher in selecting books for her classroom library.

DALE, EDGAR. *Audio-Visual Methods in Teaching (rev. ed.)*. New York, Dryden, 1954. No one should attempt to teach in elementary school without a copy of this book on his desk. It contains ideas, source materials, and methods to enrich any subject in the curriculum.

FENNER, PHYLLIS. *Something Shared: Children and Books*. New York, John Day, 1959. A rich and rewarding experience for any teacher eager to share good books with her pupils.

Insights into Modern Mathematics. Washington, D.C. National Council of Teachers of Mathematics, 23rd Yearbook, 1957. Contains discussion of the mathematics behind the suggested changes in elementary and secondary curricula.

JAMESON, MARSHALL C., and HICKS, WM. VERNON. *Elementary School Curriculum from Theory to Practice*. New York, American Book, 1960. All nineteen chapters of this book contain practical advice on elementary teaching methods and tools and techniques for evaluating results.

MIEL, ALICE, ed. *Individualizing Reading Practices*. New York, Teachers College, Columbia Univ., 1958. In the first chapter of this booklet are given criteria for record-keeping that would make a teacher feel more secure in her daily planning for and reporting on pupil progress. The remainder of the text cites specific classroom procedures at various grade levels where individualized reading is the type of instruction being employed.

SAWARDS, G. WESLEY, and SCOBEY, MARY MARGARET. *The Changing Curriculum and the Elementary Teacher*. San Francisco, Wadsworth, 1961. This text gives a comprehensive treatment of the elementary school curriculum, guides for planning, learning areas, materials, teacher's role, and evaluation.

STUART, FRANCES R. *Classroom Activities*. Washington, D.C., American Assoc. for Health, Physical Education & Recreation, 1956. The title of this pamphlet is well chosen, as it provides suggestions for quiet and active games, story plays, and other activities suitable for various grade levels from kindergarten through sixth grade. The list of source materials, films, and books would help any teacher provide a richer program for her class.

SWAIN, ROBERT L. *Understanding Arithmetic*. New York, Holt, Rinehart, Winston, 1957. An introduction to set language and a discussion of the mathematical nature of arithmetic.

VEATCH, JEANETTE. *Individualizing Your Reading Program*. New York, Putnam, 1959. Part I of this text gives a vivid description of the program and the underlying philosophy of individualized reading instruction. Part II gives us an opportunity to glimpse the program in action in various schools and at different grade levels.